GLOBAL TRAJECTORIES

GLOBAL TRAJECTORIES

Jason K. Johnson
306090 04 > Editor

Nataly Gattegno
306090 04 > Assistant Editor

306090, INC.

Alexander F. Briseno
Jonathan D. Solomon
Series Editors and Publishers

Emily A. Abruzzo
Melissa Gronlund
Editors

Thanks to:

Minna Guillermo   Ronald Weiss
Grace Ahn   Kevin Lippert
Yuki Sakamoto   Penny Chu
Cara Soh   Nettie Aljian
Brian Lemond   John Wagner

306090 > Advisory Board:

Paul Lewis   M. Christine Boyer

Michael Sorkin   Mario Gandelsonas

Christian Unverzagt   David L. Hays

Sarah Whiting   Mark Jarzombek

306090 is an independent architectural journal published and distributed biannually. 306090 seeks to publish diverse, inquisitive projects by students and young professionals that have not been published elsewhere.

Opinions expressed in 306090 are the author's alone and do not necessarily reflect those of the editors.

Distributed By:

Princeton Architectural Press
37 East Seventh Street
New York, NY 10003
1.800.722.6657
www.papress.com

www.306090.org   info@306090.org

306090, Inc. is a non-profit institution registered in the state of New Jersey and the state of New York. Your donations are tax deductible. For information on how to contribute or for ordering information please contact us at: info@306090.org or visit our Website.

05 04 03 02 5 4 3 2 1 First Edition
ISBN 1-56898-406-5

© Copyright 2003, 306090, Inc.

Cover Design: John Wagner
www.workstudios.net

Credit: Cover graphic based on the "Walrus Internet Map", CAIDA (Cooperative Association for Internet Data Analysis), © 2002 UC Regents, University of California.

306090, Inc.
350 Canal Street
Box 2092
New York, NY 10013-0875

306090 04 03 | 03

GLOBAL
TRAJECTORIES

306090 04 Guest Editorial

by Jason K. Johnson

Baghdad burns in real time. The global population accelerates toward the seven billion mark. Protesters rally in the streets—from Karachi to Sao Paulo to Lagos. The third world is ravaged by an incurable epidemic. Information is constant. Distance is negligible. Sprawl continues its slow march across vast territories, as the world gets hotter, denser, and more noxious by the day. Mesmerized by media and intoxicated by technological progress, architecture pushes forward.

This is the context from which this issue emerges. It is an expanded field of unprecedented complexity, interconnectedness and potential. Accordingly, the work collected here does not conform to any classifiable movement or distinct theoretical faction. Rather, these projects share an informed optimism, global insight, and an intellectual rigor rarely found in the field of architecture today.

This issue brings together a diverse assemblage of people, projects and interests—work by activists, academics, students and philosophers—juxtaposing the high-tech with the low-tech and the satire with the idealistic manifesto. The projects are a mix of the humanitarian, the ecological, the scientific, the theoretical and the aesthetic. In many ways these interests are connected, and if there is an affinity it is in the collective acknowledgement that these interests are fundamentally intertwined and inter-dependent. In assembling these projects, we are suggesting that cities, landscapes and ideas are in a state of perpetual global flux, and that any attempt to consider them in isolation is hopeless.

The *global trajectories* explored here might best be understood as threads—weaving, stitching and integrating ideas and meaning into the formation of our environments. Similar to any dynamic process, these threads of architecture are fleeting, ephemeral, and ultimately subject to entropy. Nothing is fixed. Nothing is isolated. Everything is transient and changing. Everything is interconnected and open-ended. One can observe this lattice-like dynamism in the projects and thoughts published here—from activated masses and global nomads, to explorations in urban interaction and trans-continental migration.

These projects raise as many questions as they begin to address: What are the cities of the future? How will these agglomerations be organized, and by whom? In what ways will these changes affect our sense of being, belonging and evolving? Ultimately, these questions will require architecture to engage an indeterminate world paralyzed by indifference and ignorance, yet empowered by scientific discovery, innovation and boundless creativity.

This is issue four.

306090 04 03 | 03

pp. 6-7 "GLOBAL TRAJECTORIES" ©2003 Jason K. Johnson, Published by 306090, Inc.

CROWDSCAPE :

THE RAVERS

Every July since 1989, a crowd has gathered in Berlin to form what is known as The Loveparade. Over the years the popularity of this event has grown exponentially. In 1989 there were 150 participants; by 1999, 1.5 million people joined the celebration. Touted as "a peaceful demonstration for a rave population," this happening has spawned similar events in Leeds, Vienna, Tel Aviv and Cape Town.

THE BROTHERS

Power in numbers was the undeniable inspiration behind the Million Man March in 1995. The aptly named march was intended to bring over one million black men to Washington, D.C., increasing the population of the city by 50% in one day. The estimated size of the crowd was hotly debated, ranging from 400,000 attendees to an incredible 1.5 million, depending on sources. The official head count, conducted by Dr. Farouk El-Baz of Boston University, was settled at 837,000.

306090 04. 03 | 03

pp. 08–17 "CROWDSCAPE" ©2003 Chloe Town, Published by 306090, Inc.

Whether people gather to pray, protest or shop, the basic fact remains: we must make room for the crowd

THE MASS PROGRAM

by Chloe Town

Chloe Town received her MArch in 2002 from Princeton University. Since moving from New Jersey to Brooklyn, New York she has co-founded Parallel City, a collaboration exploring architecture through urbanism.

Contact: parallel.city@verizon.net

THE BATHERS

On January 24, 2001, the most populous city in the world was not Tokyo, Mumbia or Lagos but Allahabad, India. On that day—as Hindis celebrated the most auspicious day of Kumbh Mela with a spiritual cleansing in the Ganges—more people gathered in one place on Earth than has ever been recorded before. The 24 square mile city ballooned to 30 million people. It was as if the entire state of California relocated itself to the city of Pasadena.

CROWDS + ARCHITECTURE

The term *public space* goes in and out of fashion in architectural discourse. Judging from the World Trade Center redesign presentations in January 2003, now the expression is very much *in* again. Even though the teams have had less than half an hour to present their work, each managed to talk at length about spaces dedicated to the public. It was as if the very utterance of *public* added credibility to their schemes. The popularity of this word could not have gone unnoticed. With a nod to civic consciousness, we were promised public plazas, public memorials and public sky-gardens. But what does this qualifier say, if anything, about form-making?

It is not surprising that architects would offer public space; what is unusual is their assumption that we, the public, had understood what they meant. Were they advocating for space that is accessible to all, at all times? Inviting the public into what is essentially private property is seldom simple. In this case, it is especially complicated. The hours of occupancy would most likely be limited, activities monitored and the size of gatherings curtailed. Jerold Kayden's thorough assessment of over 500 of New York's privately owned public spaces provides poignant evidence that public spaces owned and operated by private developers are quite unlike public streets, sidewalks and parks[1]. Seldom monitored for

306090 04 03 | 03

efficacy, the city's existing privately owned public spaces are highly undesirable destinations in all too many instances, with no direct sunlight, natural vegetation or places to sit. A few are blocked off from users entirely. New York's1961 zoning resolution that gave developers increased height allowance in return for maintaining public plazas has been no boon. The city has been left with scattered and inconsequential pockets of public space.

Given the fact that public and private space in cities are increasingly indistinguishable from one another (particularly in North America), pressure mounts on conscientious architects, politicians and developers to be more specific about the intention of occupancy. It is careless to confuse open space with public space. Open space describes a physical condition. It is not ideologically determined. Public space, on the other hand, is closely wedded to the principles of democracy. At the very least, it suggests a belief in social equality. (Now that the term *public space* has been whittled down to the acerbic formula "shopping=public space,"[2] the conceptual certainty of this term has been seriously undermined.)

What binds both popular malls and the WTC site is more than this loose notion of public space. In physical terms, both share the performative virtue of attracting a great number of people to one place. That is, regardless of the difference in program, these spaces function as compressors. They have the potential to turn the individual into a mass. And it is here that we encounter one of the most pressing physical and material realities of architecture today: the crowd.

Crowds have numerous architectural and urban implications—from inner-city riots to Disney World, mass migration to Civil Rights protests—yet they have surprisingly few contemporary theorists. Not since Elias Canetti wrote *Crowds and Power* in 1960 has the subject been closely examined. And he had little to say about the relationship that crowds have to buildings. In fact, from the earliest texts onwards, attention has focused almost exclusively on the psychological implications of group dynamics. Gustave Le Bon (1841-1931), the first to write about the topic at length, warned about the dangers—what he called the "delusions and madness"—of crowds. He pointed out that large groups of people act as a unified organism rather than as individuals; his idea was soon adopted by biologists.[3] To architects and urban planners, however, Le Bon's observation seemed to prove that crowds required dispersion. The story of modernism is subtly inflected by the ideal of expansive, monumental space. Haussmann, Le Corbusier and Robert Moses all endeavored to build city cores that defied congestion.

Today, Paris and New York are still teeming with people, and there are many more cities with far greater populations. Architecture, it turns out, does not fundamentally diffuse. It congeals. If anything, as the human population continues to escalate and cities grow ever larger, crowds have become inevitable. Despite television, despite the Internet, we still do many things together, in the flesh, en masse. In populous urban centers throughout the world, crowds provide a physical filter through which we experience space. It makes little difference whether we like crowds or not. What matters is that we look beyond program (a theme park, a transportation hub, a nightclub) to recognize the potential of crowds to transform space. A crowd takes up space at the same time as it defines it. To paraphrase McLuhan: the mass is the message.

< Crowdscape model

pp. 08-17 "CROWDSCAPE" @2003 Chloe Town, Published by 306090, Inc.

MASS CONVERGENCE

The largest gathering of humans ever recorded took place a few years ago, in India, in January 2001. Over the course of a six-week period, 25 million people converged on the city of Allahabad. The degree of organization required to stage such an event was staggering. State officials spent months preparing to accommodate the masses. They laid a street and electrical grid on a flood plane. In effect, a temporary city of eighteen square miles was built out of canvas and bamboo tents, knowing that only a few months later it would all have to be removed.

Such spectacular events are becoming increasingly common worldwide. On a smaller scale, they are no less breathtaking. In Berlin, what started as a modest celebration three months after the collapse of the Berlin wall swelled to a 1.5-million-person happening by 1999. Every year, millions of Muslims make their way to Mecca as part of the haj pilgrimage. In Detroit, tens of thousands of people congregate annually in this otherwise depopulating city as part of an electronic music festival. In Indianapolis, hundreds of thousands of people watch the Indy500 car race every May. In New York City, 30,000 people run a marathon through the city's five boroughs every fall while two-million more watch along the course.

In each of these instances, the potential of the crowd to change its form, to transmogrify, is perhaps its single most significant quality. Yet the spatial impact of these crowds cannot be separated from the technologies that make such large human gatherings possible. In addition to modern advances in transportation,[4] contemporary communication technologies essentially guarantee the cohesion of crowds. The advent of voice amplification at the start of the 20th century, for example, allowed for the transmission of sound across greater physical distances. Large-scale outdoor assemblies, such as Woodstock, or those people amassed beyond the steps of the Lincoln Memorial on August 28, 1963,[5] demonstrate the impact that audio technologies have had on contemporary culture. Similarly, Jumbotrons and large format projections have diminished the need for immediate sightlines. Most recently, handheld communication devices, such as cell phones and PDAs, have now made smart crowds possible. The anti-globalization protestors in Seattle in December 1999 demonstrated the surprising agility of crowds today: highly informed mobile gatherings can swarm and dissipate at a moment's notice.

The symbolic resonance of extra-large groups of people has a lot to do with the consumption of space. The antiwar demonstrations on February 15, 2003—attended by millions of people in cities around the world—were a physical manifestation of discontent. Aerial images of this mass demonstration show cities besieged with bodies. Thus, form was given to invisible political and

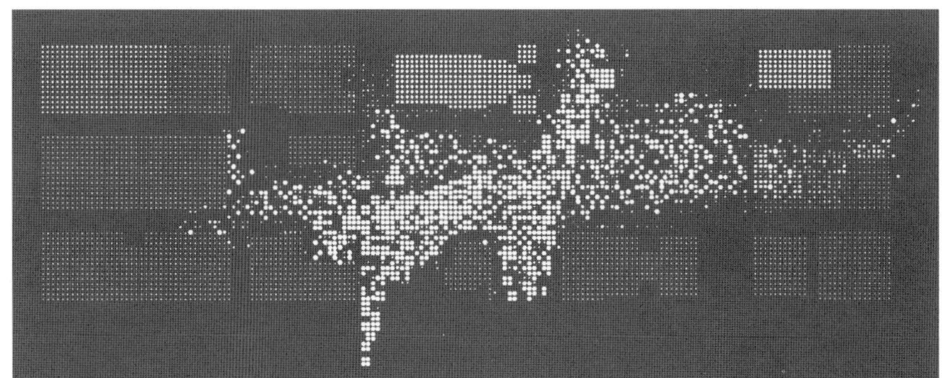

social desires. In New York City, however, the police maintained barricades along Third Avenue (under the guise of a security precaution) to prevent thousands of demonstrators from joining the larger rally on First Avenue. In frustration, a sudden shift in ideology swept through the crowd. People were soon shouting *Our city, our streets!* in futile retaliation. The politics of the occupancy of public space had come to the fore precisely because of the size of the gathering. By dispersing participants, the total area of the crowd was significantly reduced. Thus the police had prevented both the immediate gathering and its legacy. Since photographers could not document a cohesive crowd, there is no way of knowing how many people attended the event.[6]

The crowd-control tactics used in New York—diminishing the unified crowd—provide powerful evidence that the city is ill prepared for the future. If authorities in America's most populous city can't figure out where to put their crowds today, what will happen twenty, forty or a hundred years from now? The quandary is, in part, a fiction—millions of people could obviously assemble in Central Park. But Olmsted's intention for Central Park was entirely different. He saw the park as a safe haven from the perpetual excitement of the city. His meandering footpaths forced people to slow down and separate from one another. In any case, New York has remarkably few alternative places for large crowds to gather. The city expects too much of a grid that was designed in 1811. While it is claimed that Times Square attracted up to 2 million people during the millennium celebrations, the reality is far different. It is physically impossible to fit even half that number into the square.

What New York and every densely inhabited city needs is a place for people to gather other than the streets, other than parks. Streets are for cars; parks are a refuge from a city's congestion. In effect, a new typology is required. The challenge lies in designing for crowds in existing, densely built urban cores.

306090 04 03 | 03

pp. 08-17 "CROWDSCAPE" ©2003 Chloe Town, Published by 306090, Inc.

∧ Crowd as architectural material

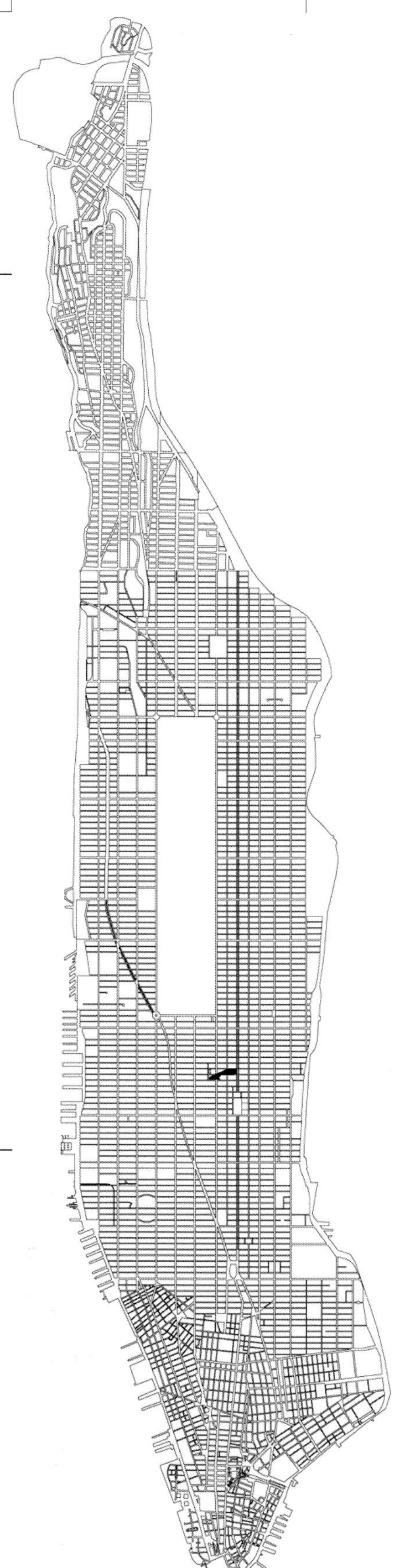

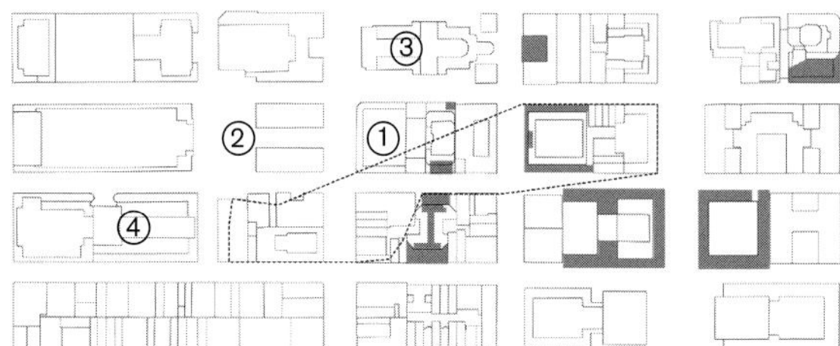

Existing Condition [existing privately owned space shaded]

① Saks ② Rockefeller Center ③ St Patricks ④ NBC Today Show

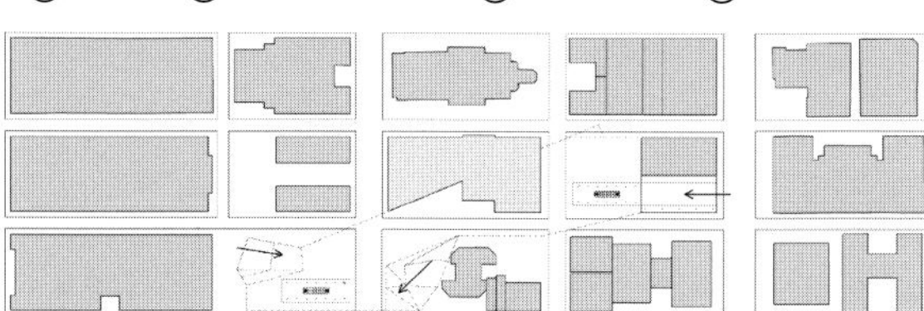

Crowdscape at 0 ft from sidewalk

three wide ramps from sidewalk 24-7 access

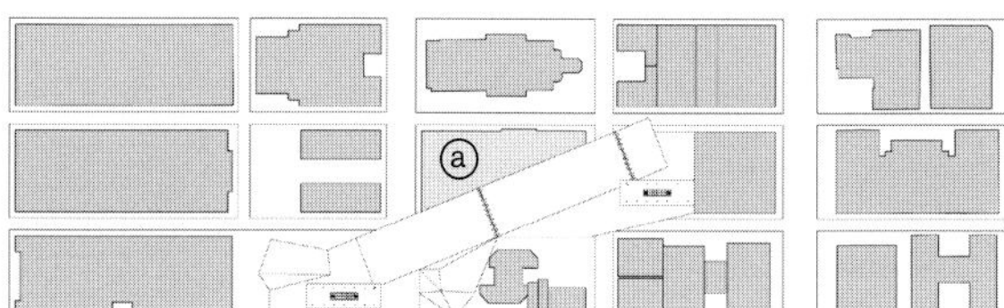

Crowdscape at 25 ft from sidewalk

ⓐ augmented building

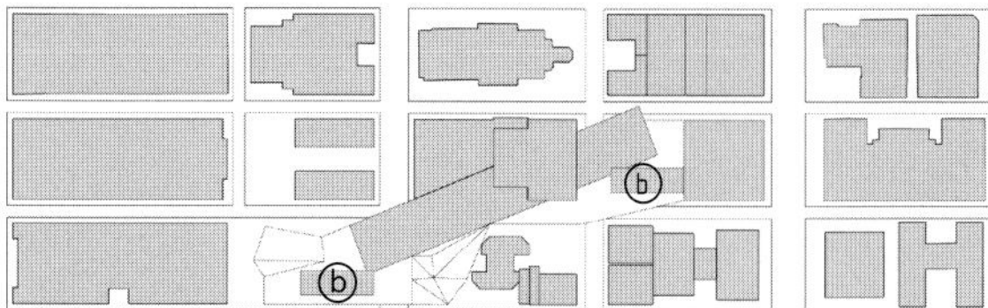

Crowdscape at 500 ft from sidewalk

ⓑ new towers

306090 04 03 | 03

pp. 08-17 "CROWDSCAPE" ©2003 Chloe Town, Published by 306090, Inc.

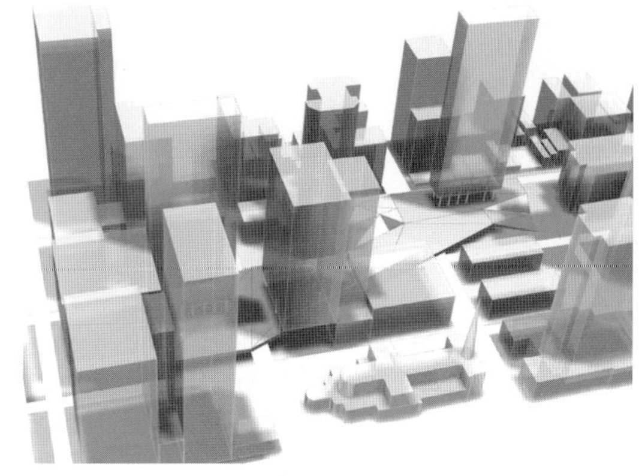

Crowdscape from 51st St looking South

CROWDSCAPE: THE MASS PROGRAM

The Crowdscape is a design concept for a place for crowds to gather. In this proposal, the Crowdscape consists of a three-block augmentation of midtown Manhattan. The site, stretching east along 49th Street from Rockefeller Center, is framed by a number of existing crowd attractors—5th Avenue shopping, St Paul's Cathedral, The Waldorf-Astoria Hotel, The MoMA, and Grand Central Station, et cetera. The Crowdscape draws from these attractors and siphons many more from the numerous towers close by. Since midtown Manhattan has the greatest concentration of tall buildings in the city, human density already exists. What the Crowdscape makes possible is the translation of extruded density (that is, people stacked floor by floor) onto a horizontal plane. In other words, the elongation of form brought on through vertical organization finds its physical counterpoint once the crowd is located along the new terrain. The Crowdscape allows for the possibility of mass convergence.

Two things distinguish the Crowdscape. First, the surface radically mediates between economic sectors. The Crowdscape expands upon the landscape of the street and avoids the monofunctional nature of commercial crowd containers. Second, the Crowdscape is less an object in a field than a prosthetic. Not only does it do away with figure-ground tradition, but it also augments existing buildings. In this scheme the footprint of Sak's Fifth Avenue is drastically reduced as the Crowdscape wends its way across the grid. Unlike Central Park, which is a vast expanse separated from the density of the city and the grid, the Crowdscape engages with the immediate surroundings of busy streets, retail space and office complexes.

Promoted as a dynamic place for large groups of people to gather, the Crowdscape is part open-air concourse, and part convergence park. Access is gained through several banks of elevators and three 75-foot wide-ramps. Two towers, 30 stories each, anchor the site and house the ancillary needs of the Crowdscape (washrooms, storage, communication technologies, etc). This hybrid terrain can support multiple activities. The Macy's Parade, Gay Lesbian Bisexual and Transgender March or the New York City Marathon could all move through this space. After a Yankees win, before an activist march or during the holiday season, large groups of people (up to 100,000 on the surface alone) could gather at the site. The Crowdscape could also be used in times of emergency.

In each of these instances, the mass is the program.

ACCOMMODATING THE FUTURE

During the Victorian era, architecture was promoted as a means to control the spatial organization of people. In 1862, Richard Owen, the curator of London's National Museum of History, argued that museums were the best means to stave off revolution in England. He characterized museums as "a safety valve, an elaborate crowd control device."[7] Later in the 20th century, however, we learned from Foucault that power transcends built form.

If cities are going to physically evolve in a way that is analogous to cultural change, we need to continually assess the new ways that urban and architectural space is actually used. It is futile, for example, to simply build bigger and bigger buildings because our populations are growing larger and larger. Despite Hans Ibeling's seductive examination of "supermodernism,"[8] container spaces can only grow so big before they cease to be successful. People will only sit so far out in the bleachers. Extra-large container spaces, such as train stations or sport stadiums, need to be studied with the certainty of crowds in mind.

Forming inside stadiums and airports, on street corners and subway platforms, crowds permeate our physical world. Whether people gather to pray, protest or shop, the basic fact remains: we must make room for the crowd. A Crowdscape is conceived with a possibility for density in mind.

It provides a space where crowds can collect, expand and disperse at will, ensuring the free movement of people elsewhere in the city. Thus, a Crowdscape reciprocates our desire for general dispersion with a site-specific design for convergence.

End Notes:

[1] Jarold Kayden, The New York City Department of City Planning and The Municipal Art Society of New York, "Privately Owned Public Space: The New York Experience", John Wiley and Sons, 2000.

[2] Rem Koolhaas, "Harvard Project on the City", in Mutatiions, ACTAR, arc en reve, centre d'architecture, Barcelona + Bordeaux, 2001, p 155.

[3] In 1911 William Morton Wheeler (1865-1937), claimed that insect colonies were not simply analogous to the organism, they were the organism.

[4] Planes, trains and automobiles have all contributed to the sprawl of cities and the promise of seemingly limitless human mobility.

[5] On this day Martin Luther King Jr. delivered his speech "I Have a Dream."

[6] Methods used to record the size of crowds remain surprisingly inaccurate. The default technique is to count heads from an aerial photograph.

[7] Barbara J. Black, "On Exhibit: Victorians and Their Museums", Charlottesville and London, University of Virginia Press, 2000.

[8] Hans Ibelings, "Supermodernism: Architecture in the Age of Globalization", Rotterdam, NAi Publishers, 1998.

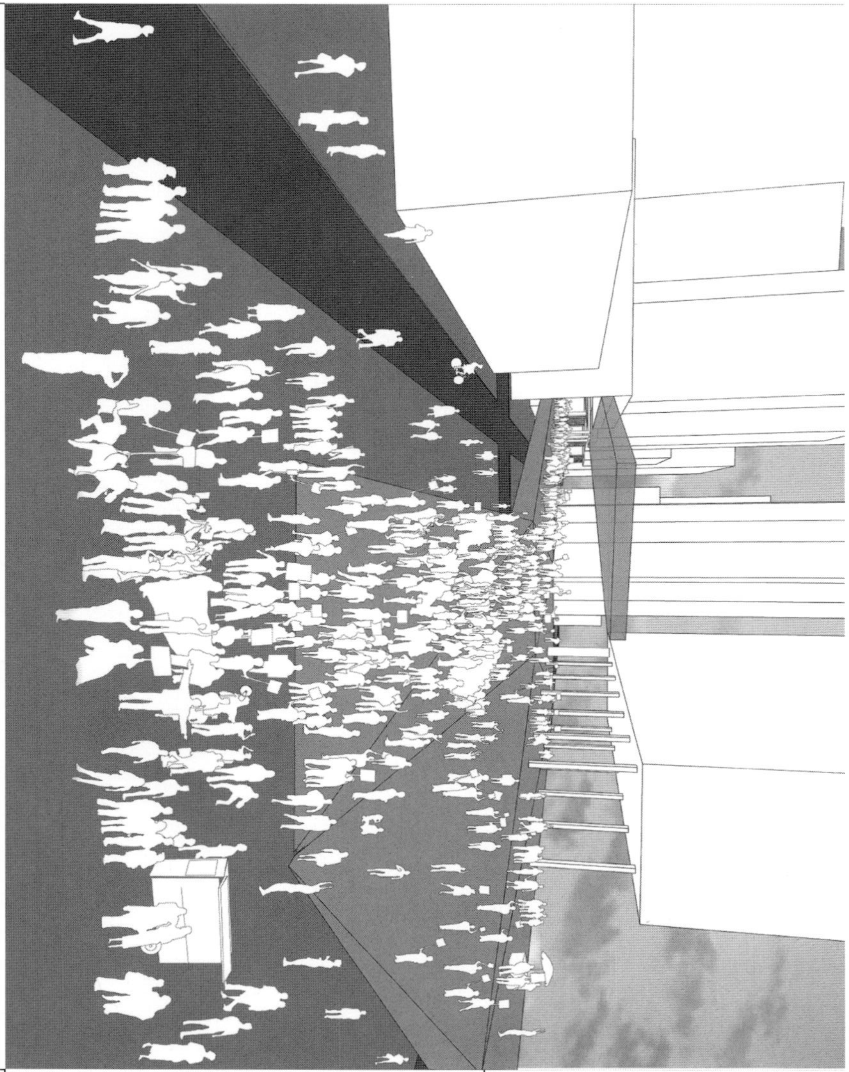

306090 04 03 | 03

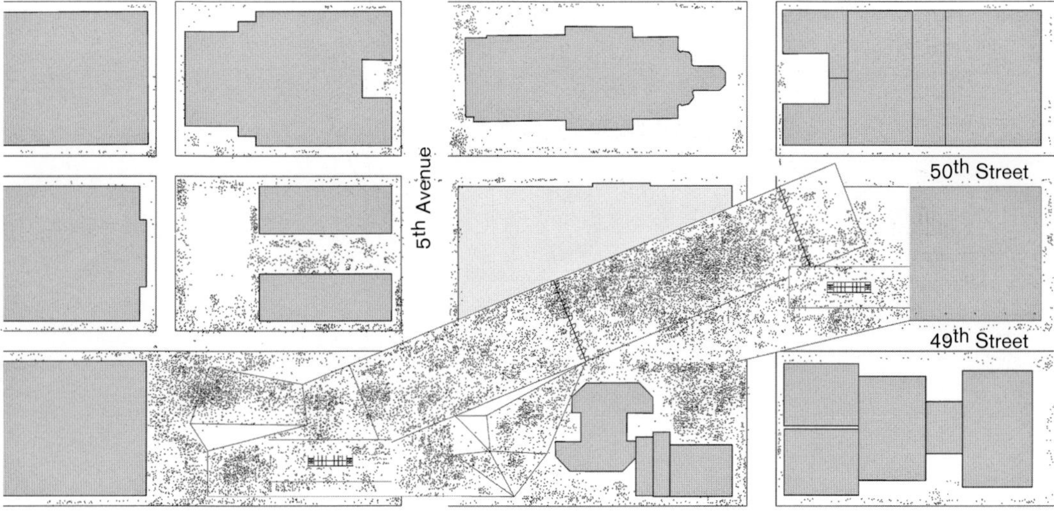

pp. 08-17 "CROWDSCAPE" ©2003 Chloe Town, Published by 306090, Inc.

⟨ Terrain for mass convergence Crowdscape: plan ⟩

THE WORLD

WHO GETS IT AND WHO WANTS IT?

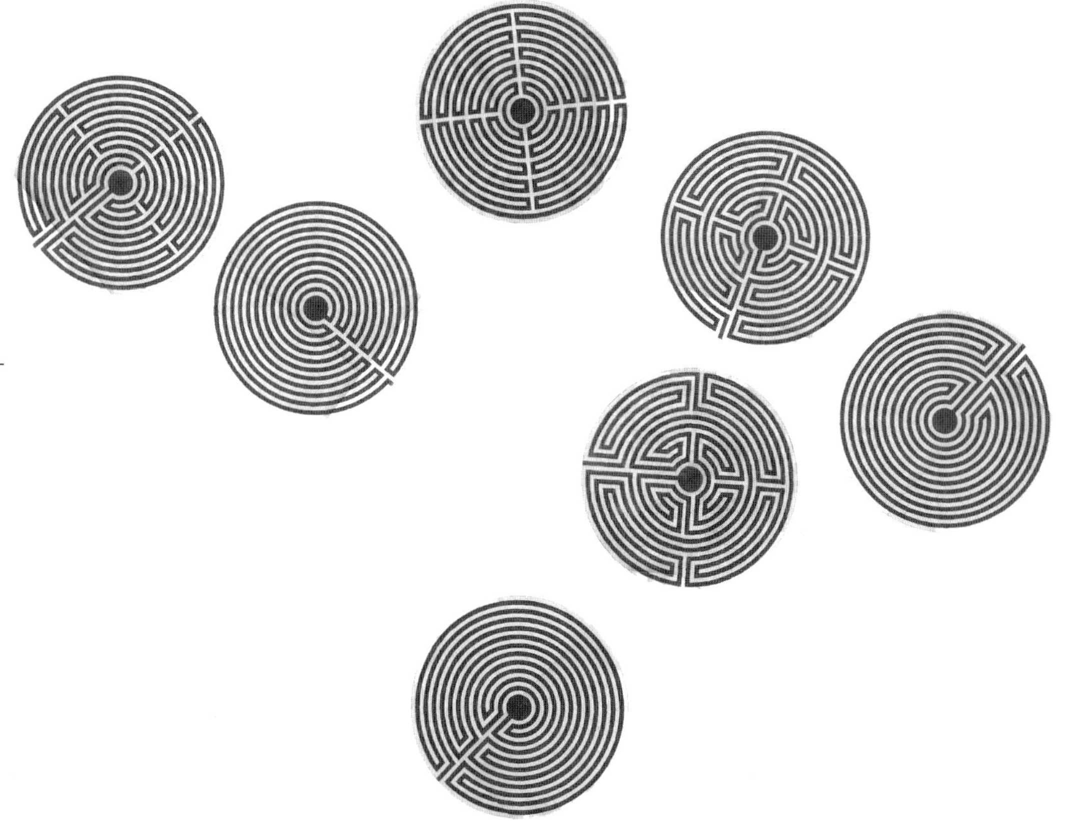

Urbs Americana

by Ben Nicholson

Urbs Americana: New York City

New York City, naturally adverse to any sort of handout from the Federal Government, will build and pay for an entirely new building type to replace the World Trade Towers. In an act of supreme generosity, New York gives Newark, New Jersey the Federal monies to build a new financial center for the world. New York passes the mantle of being the fiscal center of the Free World on to its natural sparring partner, in preference for a higher calling that is in keeping with New York's intrinsic, unpredictable sense of self-preservation and dignity.

Outside of the appalling death and destruction of the urban apocalypse, the haunting specter we are left with is that the disaster created a micro-weather system of bureaucracy and swirling winds of sheet rock dust intermingled with flakes of paper, bearing inconsequential meanings from the sky. Against this backdrop, what then goes in the hole to replace this architectural holocaust, for who in their right mind would step into an elevator of another 100-floor building? New York must cede the mighty greenback to Newark, on condition that any new towers built there are designed according to the plans of Saul Steinberg.

Ben Nicholson is currently an Assistant Professor at IIT in Chicago, Illinois, where he teaches architectural design and theory. He Received his M.Arch from the Cranbrook Academy of Art. Fellowships include: The S.O.M. Foundation, The Illinois Artists Council. Exhibitions at: The Canadian Center of Architecture, Montreal; Cartier Foundation, Paris; Aedes Gallery, Berlin. Publications include: The Appliance House, the CD-Rom Thinking the Unthinkable House, and contributions to the books The Presence of Mies and Art and the Public Sphere. Current projects concern the relationship of architecture and information through an interdisciplinary examination of the book collection, architecture and geometry of Michelangelo's Laurentian Library.

Contact: nicholson@iit.edu

306090 04.03|03

pp. 18-23 "The World" ©2003 Ben Nicholson, Published by 306090, Inc.

New York is now readied to move on to greater acts of statehood, philanthropic majesty and raw power. The first hint of the change is that the WTC blocks are rezoned: a radical change of use is decreed, from it being a space dedicated to business to a space for the exercise of the quid pro quo. A hole is prepared at Ground Zero on the site between the former twin towers of the World Trade Center. This time, a shaft five hundred feet deep and having the same width as the diameter of the Dome of the Rock in Jerusalem, is cut into the granite beneath New York City. At its bottom a mold is prepared whose inner surface area exactly equals the volume of gold currently held in the United States. Once the liquid gold has been poured, the granite mold is chipped apart and a simple earth surface is prepared around the luminous ball for people to walk upon.

At ground level, a series of seven labyrinths are laid out on the sixteen-acre site, each a meditation on the nature of the path between the outside and the inside, between the self and the goal. Around the hole in which resides the Fed's bullion ball, a stone parapet is built at its rim for visitors to stare down at the marvel of accumulated wealth glowing at the bottom of the hole. A double spiral staircase winds around the sidewall of the hole, permitting access to the sphere from the earth's surface. A shaft is sunk beside the hole into which is inserted an elevator for the use by the infirm, and made available to those who present the necessary credentials. There is no need for any security whatsoever, as it is impossible to remove the bullion ball due to its staggering weight and unstable mobility.

Visitors are welcome to visit the bullion sphere on the condition that they are completely naked by the time they reach the base of the hole. Pilgrims of wealth discard their clothing while they walk, run or stumble down the ramp, throwing clothing and accessories in heaps onto the pavement, thus removing the desire for theft or the will to scratch initials on the ball with a solitaire diamond. The naked humans spread-eagle themselves against this icon of materialism, some frantically baring their teeth in a desperate attempt to have some of the National Wealth or at least be able to leave their mark upon it. Once satiated by the mesmerizing power of the bullion ball, the naked forms stagger or dreamily glide up the ramp, scrambling over clots of Cartier bracelets and Prada footwear intertwined with cheap acrylic sweatshirts distributed by Wal-mart. Blinded by gold, the folly of ownership, uncaring to determine which inner and outer clothing they owned, and unconscious of the glittering accessories they once lavished so much of their income on, the visitors emerge at the rim of the hole in a daze, where they are gently taken to

one side and covered by a simple garment for the sake of public decorum.

The view from above, of telescopically diminutive figures crowding around the glowing element, is a simple yet unforgettable sight, perhaps overtaking the popularity of the Metropolitan Museum. Humanity is at last seen for what it is, a blob of reptilian creatures swarming and crawling over matter that they desperately desire to possess.

Away from this spectacle of consumerism, uptown on 42nd Street, the United Nations building closes its mission for good. The whole operation is moved to its new location on a man-made island in the newly restored Dead Sea near Jerusalem. The billionaire Mayor of New York announces that he will build a place for all the NGO's in the world, a counterpoint to organized government, called the UNGO. Every representative of any and every cause is invited to Manhattan to state their case and a new era of understanding is born. New York reestablishes its *enfant terrible* reputation but this time that quality is safely institutionalized in UNGO, an organization created to go against the grain and make the 'voice of the little guy' audible from a distance. New York it is the center of it all, as she takes on the persona of enveloping political correctness at the international level.

Lastly, the precariously leaning wall of the old World Trade Center is welded back together and set up exactly where it was. It imitates the Dome left standing at ground zero where the Americans detonated a nuclear device in the midst of Hiroshima, that other marker of inhuman atrocity against an unknowing civilian population. The WTC monument would simply show how technology can be turned against itself, duplicating the central tenet of Aikido in which the power generated by the one is channeled by the other to go against itself. This monument serves to show the world the sting of technology's tail, the dangerous construct of hubris, in which the works of humankind can get horribly out of control, challenging their own seemingly inviolable circle in a scenario that only the Greek polytheistic writers acknowledged the dangers of and had the skill to express.

New York now fills out its boots, a senior city that has grown to a new stature, no longer alive to its own youth but joyful in maturity and content in its recurring memories. New York joins the ranks of the once glorious cities of London, Shanghai, Rome, Kabul, Florence and Moscow. Just as we now go to Florence to see the marvels of the Renaissance, we now visit New York to see the marvels of Capitalism, a place where everything from culture to

Development of the World

During 2001-2002, this satire was written conjuring up a spectacle of America's imperialist tendencies. It developed into a vision for how the country can maintain its position with dignity through the implementation of performative artistry and architecture. The text was part of an exhibition about the rebuilding of the World Trade Center, staged by Max Protetch, which represented America at the 2002 Venice Biennale of Architecture. It has recently been acquired by the United States National Archive.

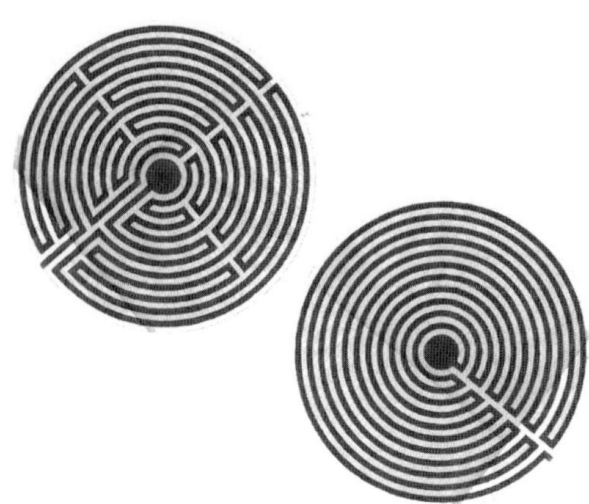

The first part of the satire describes the Bilateral Peace Corps, a federally funded international program which brings back American Values in the guise of former 1960's recipients of the Peace Corps program. They set up cells in the meeting places of Twelve Step Programs and then fan out across the country, teaching Americans how to appreciate simple pleasures in a distended hyper-technological culture. Once Americans have regained the principles of nutrition, clothing & possessions, transport, health & housing, the BPC hands off the responsibility of running the country to its citizens.

The second section outlines a complete restructure of the Federal Government, making provision for new agencies that regulate and give form to the new society. The aim of the new administration is to reestablish social justice by showing the nature of reality. Traditional divisions of government are abandoned and are replaced with new agencies and events that respond directly to the needs of the country. Some of the named agencies are; The Birth & Control Board, The Food & Packaging Administration, Drug Administration, Extrascriptual Law, Real & Native Americans and a host of other active agencies. The line between philanthropic provision and misanthropic control finds itself being constantly criss-crossed as the new order struggles for direction.

The third part of the text deals with international policy and cuts to the quick by focusing on the rebuilding of the City of Jerusalem, under the watchful protection of America. All the hopes and aspirations of the three Abrahamic faiths are accommodated in a harmonious display of architectural wherewithal. Beginning with the construction of a new Pilgrim Airport built in the Gaza Strip, it goes on to describe a burial ground for strands of DNA around the Old City, thus permitting internment for all. The Temple Mount is reconfigured and renamed Tabula Rasa: a complex of architectural and landscaping solutions are built upon it that give form to the harmonious integration of Judaism, Christianity and Islam. The centerpiece is a new setting for the Rock of Saqhra and allocates the air rights to the Muslim community and the land rights to the Jewish body. The whole spectacle is over-looked by a new church, built to heal the three great rifts of Christianity. With this essential task accomplished, America goes on to establish and defend Religious Freedom for the inhabitants of the world, thus bringing it's revered Constitution to the population of the globe.

The text then positions America in a Post Constitutional Age in which the concept of religious freedom collapses. A national cause is set in place to reenact the Book of Revelation, to perpetrate the return of the Messiah through sheer will. A 1:10 scale model of the New Jerusalem is built in the Sun Belt, a retirement community for 144,000.

306090 04 03 | 03

pp. 18-23 "The World" ©2003 Ben Nicholson, Published by 306090, Inc.

Labyrinths >

The Golden Ball >

306090 04 03 | 03

pp. 18-23 "The World" ©2003 Ben Nicholson, Published by 306090, Inc.

nourishment was bought for hard cash, and which attracted colonies of artists who produced things and thoughts to reflect this quirky opulence. In the same way that art historians flock to Florence to create beautiful, studied drawings in the manner of the masters, coached by tweedy professors with British accents, students of art will come to New York to bathe in the culture of its golden years. In the summer months effete students of art erratically flick paint at oversized canvasses while an adoring daddy stands by, happy to have been able to give his darling daughter the culture that he wants and she has learned to crave.

Ezekiel's vision of Jerusalem the Whore.
> *They shall bring up a mob against you and they shall stone you and cut you in pieces with swords. They shall burn your houses and execute judgments on you in the sight of many women: I will stop you from playing the whore... (Ezekiel 16: 40-41)*

Muhammad, on a Sinful City.
> *When we resolve to raze a city, we first give warning to those of its people who live in its comfort. If they persist in sin, judgment is irrevocably passed and we destroy it utterly (Sura 17:16).*

Evangelical Christian scholars on the Book of Revelations.
> *The city: the social and political embodiment of human self-sufficiency and rebellion against God. (Sweet) The city: the mounting structure of human arrogance which defies the authority of Almighty God (Hughes) (Robert Mounce, The Book of Revelation, page 221.)*

ENGAGING UTOPIA:

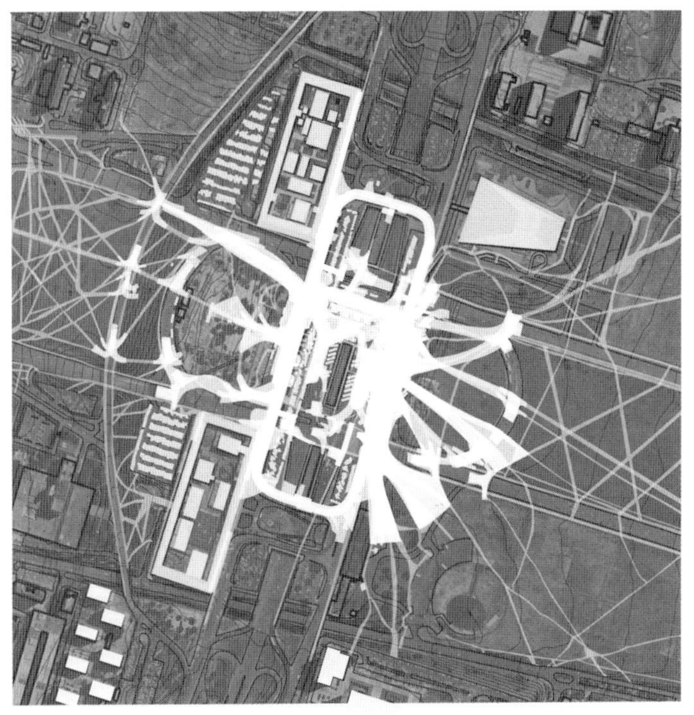

306090 04 03 | 03

pp. 24-29 "Engaging Utopia" ©2003 Mark Rakatansky et al, Published by 306090, Inc.

A joint studio at Columbia University investigates global culture in the capital city of Brasilia

LOCALIZING GLOBALISM

by Mark Rakatansky (with Sunil Bald) and Paul Spencer Byard

Brief History of the Program

Columbia's Joint Third Year Advanced Design Studio/Historic Preservation Workshop is the leading component of a pioneering initiative of the Graduate School of Architecture Planning & Preservation to combine designers and preservationists. This program provides the unusual chance for the most advanced architecture and historic preservation studetns to collaborate in a highly demanding design and historic environment.

Similarly, the studio combines the various and varied interests of several faculty; Sunil Bald's interest in the role of the mythologies and narratives that bind modern architecture to the nation-making process in Brazil; Paul Byard's aim to reinvigorate the field of historic preservation by developing innovative design and preservation techniques to advance architecture within historic contexts; and Mark Rakatansky's developments in the performative play of architectural elements as characters enacting the social and psychological and political dramas of institutional space.

In previous years, the school raised similar questions in design with Chandigahr in India (Laurie Hawkinson, Kadambari Baxi and Paul Byard) and the Universidad Autonomo Nacional de Mexico in Mexico City (Katherine Dean and Paul Byard), exploring the ways new architecture can collaborate with old masterworks—even the most difficult of them—and put them to work to meet critical contemporary needs.

COLUMBIA UNIVERSITY GRADUATE SCHOOL OF ARCHITECTURE PLANNING AND PRESERVATION

Joint Third Year Advanced Design Studio and Historic Preservation Workshop—Fall 2002

MARK RAKATANSKY is principal of Mark Rakatansky Studio. His work and writing has been published in a wide variety of publications in the United States, Europe, and Asia. Mark teaches design studios and theory seminars at Columbia University.

SUNIL BALD: Adjunct Assistant Professor of Architecture B.A., University of California Santa Cruz, 1986; MArch, Columbia, 1991. A.I.A. Medal, 1991; Fulbright Fellow, Architectural League of New York, 1999.

PAUL SPENCER BYARD: Adjunct Associate Professor of Historic Preservation; Director, Historic Preservation Program B.A., Yale, 1961; B.A., Cambridge, 1963; L.L.B., Harvard, 1966; M.A., Cambridge, 1968; MArch, Columbia, 1977. Director, Architectural League of New York; New York Landmarks Conservancy; Vinmont Foundation; American Friends of Cambridge University. Fellow, A.I.A. Registered architect.

Architecture Students:

Christopher Barker	*Yi-Wei Chang***	*John Chuang*
I-Shin Chow	*Tobie Cornejo*	*Daniela Fabricius*
Jennifer Gellin	*Shan-Cheng Kao***	*Beatriz Nadal*
Jee Young Park	*Andre Soluri***	*Amparo Vollert*

Historic Preservation Students:

Courtney Flint	*Sarah Garlinghouse*	*Margaret Minard*
*Roxanne Ryce-Paul**	*Erik Sigge*	*Cara Soh*
Emily Thompson	*Deborah Van Steen*	*Takushi Yoshida*

Darrin Krumpus, Teaching Assitant
**Also Urban Planning   **Advanced Architectural Design*

Constructed in the late 1950s and early 1960s, Brasilia represents the most extensive mid-twentieth century social experiment with architecture. Planned by Lucio Costa and designed by Oscar Niemeyer for Juscelino Kubitschek, the progressive President of Brazil, Brasilia built out the idea of the modern city, including its proposed leap forward to a new egalitarian social order beyond bourgeois capitalism. The result of the leap is a design of great formal and social power and, at the same time, extreme formal and social awkwardness—provisions for ordinary bourgeois social interaction beyond the modernists' canonical housing, work, recreation and traffic having been leapt over and left out in a deliberate effort to jump start an egalitarian dream. The architecture of Brasilia still points to the possibility of a different social future.

Given the obvious relevance of Neimeyer's experiments in geometries and responses to problems of *bigness*, a revisitation of a great *would-be* model is timely—an opportunity to get beyond too-easy assumptions about its failure to a recognition of sources and continuing potential. Tafuri's relatively generous critique of the buildings of Brasilia—"in these the gratuitous is tinged with sophistication"[1]—reflected Neimeyer's difficulty in enlarging his previous smaller scaled sophistications of tectonics, processions, massings and meanings to the scale of a global capital, with results that seem alternately over—and under-blown. The students involved in this workshop attempted to learn from Brasilia where the dynamic is dynamic (and where it becomes static) and likewise, where the static remains static (and where it can become dynamic).

The context of Brazil provides many nuanced examples of Niemeyer's work—especially in Rio de Janiero and Pampulha—that allow for an understanding of what our own localized globalism will struggle with when the programs intervene in the capitol. As with Brazilian music, we will analyze and design with the tectonic and programmatic beats and counter beats of order and improvisation, global and local, structure and lyric. The integration of students allowed for a deeper understanding of Brasilia's design and built history and logic. This analysis of existing conditions and the city's architectural and urban strategies allowed the students to arrive at design proposals that demonstrate how the now-new and the then-new can interact in engaging ways.

The program, a new headquarters for the World Social Forum, seeks to explore problems of global reach and local impact like those originally addressed by Brasilia. Rapidly becoming the most important consortium of social awareness and action on the left, the Forum is a diversified association of political groups and grass-roots organizations from around the world seeking to move beyond generalized liberal politics and automatic anti-globalism, to new highly democratic engagements that might make possible the *different world* of its motto.

The student proposals offer the Forum a focus for its global activities in a major new development in Brasilia. The new venue offers a seat for the Forum's creative thinking and a venue for its interaction with important governments. It will enrich the modern city with its permanent and visiting populations and enlist the symbolism of Brasilia's architecture and ambitions to support efforts of global reform. The design program includes venues for public assembly, conferences, a secretariat, transient and long term housing and educational facilities.

To achieve those goals one must first have an understanding of the existing architecture of Brasilia, most importantly its expression—the meaning it was originally expected to convey and the meaning it can convey today. The projects absorb Brasilia's history and existing program and the proposed program of the Forum, develop strategies for their relation and embody them in architectures that support and change in interactive ways, engaging its meaning and enabling it to lead a proposed new combination that is more than the sum of its parts—an engagement with the problems of Brasilia that may well leave, as Tafuri suggested, "the problems of the past living and unresolved, since they continue to affect (and to disturb) the present as we know it."[2]

End Notes:

[1] Manfredo Tafuri and Francesco Dal Co, Modern Architecture (New York, Abrams: 1979), p 379.

[2] Manfredo Tafuri, "A Search for Paradigms: Project, Truth, Artifice," Assemblage 28 (December 1995), p 49.

Beatriz Nadel / Cara Soh

This project attempts to reinterpret the aim of Brasilia's Modern architectural aesthetics—to break from anything that represented the historical vernacular architecture of Brasil. The project is sited to interrupt the "Three Powers" around the main governmental triangle in Brasilia. The World Social Forum sits between the National Congress (the power of ideas) and the Planalto Palace (the executive power). Certain elements from the given context were taken and reinterpereted in order to create a more personable and experiential building that would house the physical activities of the World Social Forum, which has mainly lived in cyber-space since its foundation. Like the organization of the World Social Forum, this project attempted to de-stratify given convention, without losing any ideas that have been proven to work within its context.

The use of the brise-soleil was a starting point to investigate a solid/void argument of the breaking up of space in relationship to Brasilia's architecture breaking from the vernacular. We researched the different vernacular and Modern design alternatives that existed in Brasil. This lead to discussions about the tension created between solid and void surfaces of the brise-soleil. The brise soleil became a delicate veil that established a desire to search beyond its surface of modesty. For the proposed World Social Forum, the brise-soleil actually forms part of the program where it is simultaneously the bookcases for the archive and the shading device for the building. At the same time, the building of the World Social Forum becomes the filter that allows for interaction between the Planalto Palace and the National Congress building.

The archive was the most important element. The archive creates a continual dialogue between solid and void. In emphasizing this continual shift, the bookcases were designed to contain only one book per slot, creating some "built-in" air pockets emphasizing the diversity of various book sizes, contained within a strictly regulated space. These are made up of five layers of thin perforated wood panels to create a moiré effect, even when empty—creating the effect of solids—filling in the void spaces of a very young archive. This formal move blurs the boundaries between solid and void by solidifying that which would be void—light and air—while voiding that which would be solid—built space. The wall now becomes a dematerialized background as opposed to the solidity of light that occupies the foreground in the archive.

Beatriz Nadal is a third year student in the Master of Architecture program at Columbia University. She received her BA from Princeton University with a major in Architecture and a Certificate in Latin American Studies.

Cara Soh is received her MS in Historic Preservation from Columbia University in 2003 and received her MArch from the University of Michigan in 2001.

306090 04 03 | 03

pp. 24-29 "Engaging Utopia" ©2003 Mark Rakatansky et al, Published by 306090, Inc.

Andre Soluri and Roxanne Ryce-Paul

Brasilia was designed to represent the future of a promising nation. In this Modernist vision, the population was intended to live without class distinction in vast urban parks connected by freeways which led to shopping, banking and working sectors. This utopian vision, known as the Pilot Plan, disregarded the fact that automobiles were rare in Brasil in 1961. Instead, it expected the future population to adapt accordingly.

Today Brasilia contains the highest percentage of cars of any Brazilian city, owned primarily by upper-level government officials and the white-collar workforce. The vast majority of the local workforce relies on public transportation, primarily busses. Brasilia has two bus stations: one at the edge of the original city plan, and one at the center. The central bus station, or "Rodoviaria" handles primarily local busses. The Rodoviaria is at the intersection of the Monumental Axis and the transverse Highways leading to the Superquadras in the residential sectors. The Rodoviaria is easily accessed by automobiles, but not by pedestrians. The Rodoviaria has become one of the only visible signs of life in the entire city. The people who use the Rodoviaria, however, are forced to walk through vast expanses of land to get to the station, often on dirt paths. The pedestrian population's use of the city has altered the utopian landscape, carving deep paths of red earth into the vast expanses of grass. When viewed from an aerial photograph, these paths create an alternate mapping of Brasilia's utopian vision. An analysis of how the Rodoviaria functions shows how a population subjected to totalitarian planning simultaneously uses, misuses, accepts and rejects this Modernist vision.

This reading proposes an alternate mapping of Brasilia. The mapping produced a series of diagrams that illustrate how the population variously adheres to and ignores the totalitarian planning of Brasilia. The analysis identifies various uses and identifies them, qualitatively, as cultures. The cultures identified are pedestrian, commuter, commercial, governmental, quiescence, and work. These heterogeneous cultures operate simultaneously, independently and together, to create an interwoven urban fabric not visible in any other public area of the Pilot Plan. This vibrant urban fabric is appropriate for an organization like the World Social Forum.

Individual Culture Maps

The pedestrian mapping produced the most striking re-mapping of the Rodoviaria and vicinity. This diagram shows the paths traversed by the population as they migrate to and from the Rodoviaria, while clearly demonstrating their disregard for the utopian ideal of the city. The commercial mapping shows that many of the commercial uses obey the Pilot Plan, but that within the Rodoviaria they fragment and disperse due to the many pushcarts and miscellaneous vendors that work the station. In the diagram that layers all the cultures one finds areas with an intensification of use (which read as white), and those with less use, (which read as gray).

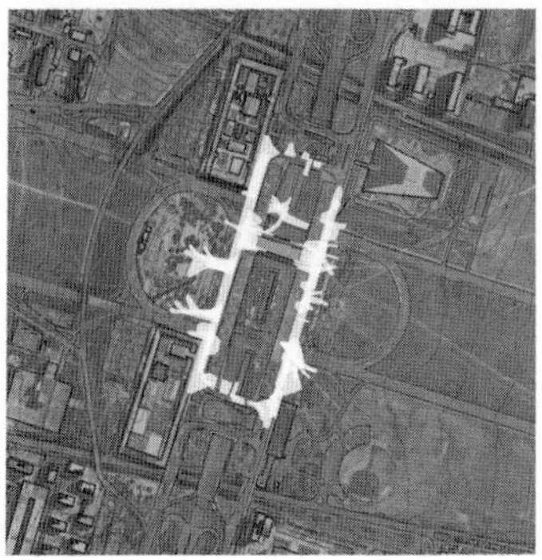

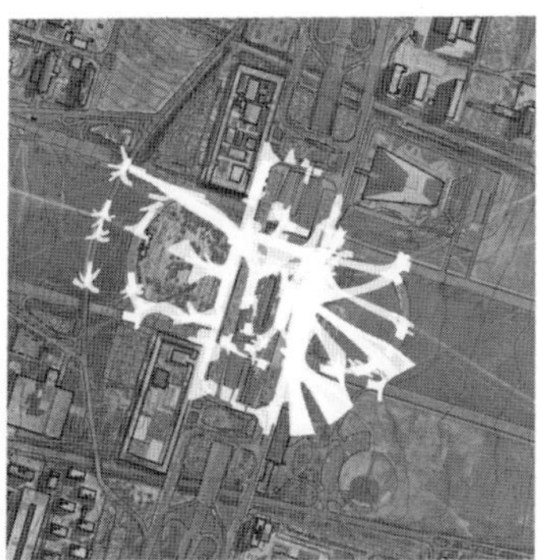

Relational Culture Maps

The individual culture mappings, which were extracted from the site, are then woven back together by determining relationships among them. These relationships can be found, for example, between pedestrian and commuter cultures; pedestrian and automobile cultures; or pedestrian and advertising cultures. The mapping of these relationships show how the individual cultures are interwoven with one another. These diagrams suggest locations for interventions into this existing fabric, as well as a methodology for (re)weaving the existing site programs with the World Social Forum.

Roxanne Ryce-Paul is currently studying Historic Preservation and Urban Planning at Columbia University. She received her BArch from the Cooper Union.

Andre Soluri is currently a Master of Science in Advanced Digital Design candidate at Columbia University. He holds a BArch from the Cooper Union and is a regular juror at Pratt Institute. He is principal of Soluri Design Group in New York City.

www.soluri.com

306090 04 03 | 03

pp. 24-29 "Engaging Utopia" ©2003 Mark Rakatansky et al, Published by 306090, Inc.

Andre Soluri

SATELLITE HOUSE

Passive Aggressive Collage / Global Nomads

A vacation home in Serbia explores conflicting ideals in transient living

by Petar Perisic

306090 04 03 | 03

pp. 30-33 "Satellite House" ©2003 Petar Perisic, Published by 306090, Inc.

The house is situated in a development along the periphery of Serbia's capital city Belgrade. The site has views of the neo-Brutalist, block-housing high-rises in the newer urban fabric of downtown as well as the military-controlled wilderness preserves. The house serves as a "satellite destination" for a trans-global Serbian-American family that was born and raised in Yugoslavia, but have been living and working in the U.S. for the last thirty years.

This project explores the obsolescence of "residing" in a single home. It advocates the move toward perpetual motion in a time-share world without borders. In addition, the house expresses the many paradoxes inherent in the Balkan situation: the dual nationalism of the client, the dueling political systems with conflicting ideologies, the coexistence of church and state under Communist rule, permanence vs. the ephemeral, the real and the virtual, the rational and the emotional. This optimistic structure serves as a reminder of more than a decade of turmoil and destruction, and pays homage to the Balkan people, both living and deceased.

SEPARATING MECHANISMS

The Satellite House aims to use communication technologies as the means to eradicate organizational separating mechanisms such as borders, walls, and containers. These mechanisms

Petar Perisic was born in Cacak, Yugoslavia in 1966. His family immigrated to the United States in 1969 and settled in a suburb of Cleveland, Ohio. In 1984, He began his formal architectural education at the Ohio State University receiving a B.S. in Architecture in 1988, and a MArch in 1991. In 1995, after several years of freelancing as a designer and architect, Perisic established his own architectural practice, Perisic Design Studio in San Diego, California.

Perisic's work has been published and exhibited internationally. He is involved in community activism as one of the leading advocates for the arts in San Diego. He is the Artistic Director for COVA (The Combined Organization for the Visual Arts) and has co-founded FLUX Gallery, an alternative art gallery, with Ken Miracle to serve as a forum and a venue for the emerging contemporary arts. He is currently working on projects in Yugoslavia, Mexico, New York, Ohio, and California. He was recently invited to present his collaborative design for a trolley station with sculptor Ante Marinovic at the international symposium III SIFFACUS, Futur I Funcio de l'Art Contemporani en l'Espai Urba, held in Barcelona, Spain and at the Urban Space Like Water exhibition.

Contact: perisic@earthlink.net

Yugoslavia has disappeared from the map of Europe after 83 years of existence to be replaced by a looser union called simply Serbia and Montenegro, after the two remaining republics.

The arrangement was reached under pressure from the European Union, which wanted to halt Montenegro's progress towards full independence. However, Montenegrin politicians say they will hold a referendum on independence in 2006.

The death of Yugoslavia is only one of many momentous changes that have occurred since the end of the Kosovo conflict. Slobodan Milosevic lost a presidential election in 2000. He refused to accept the result but was forced out of office by strikes and massive street protests, which culminated in the storming of parliament. He was handed over to a UN war crimes tribunal in The Hague and put on trial for crimes against humanity and genocide.

Kosovo itself became a UN protectorate, though some powers have begun to be handed back to elected local authorities. One of the main problems in the province is getting Serbs who fled as Yugoslav security forces withdrew in 1999 to return to their homes.

Information Source: Yugoslavia History File [http://news.bbc.co.uk]

impede interaction and communication of individuals with the rest of the world. The house was explicitly designed for the itinerant lifestyle of the global nomad. By propagating the removal of barriers, its open and ephemeral quality reflects the temporality of life and the transience of its purpose as a satellite home. Global unity might start with a dialogue; connectivity is an opportunity for this enfranchisement. Equal access to information offers us the possibility of a global democracy, and connectivity offers us unity, enlightenment, and perhaps, hope.

PARALLEL UNIVERSE

The television is an anti-memory and anti-reality device; it is a detour sign from the real to the virtual. For Americans who emigrated from Yugoslavia, the experience of watching their country of citizenship destroying their homeland was one of horror, and alienation. This evoked a complex flurry of emotions: guilt, confusion, fear, pride, humiliation, vulnerability, helplessness, and sorrow. A parallel universe emerged: For Yugoslavian immigrants, the memories they carried with them were reframed by this virtual war on TV. Stirred by the inner turmoil of disconnectedness and a sense of personal responsibility, the owners of the Satellite house are returning to their homeland with the desire

to *rebuild*. By rebuilding, they're reconnecting. The memory of their homeland is salvaged as a *dematerialized reconstruction*. This house is a space that exists in the schism between two parallel worlds: framed between the real and the virtual.

This phenomenon plagues the development of a trans-global citizenry. Many dream of returning to their native country as a form of pilgrimage, going back and forth from one side to the other. These people live in an *in-between* zone that is not entirely clear. The desire for *the other* produces a constant urge to go home. Things *over there* have changed; they are no longer the way they remember. Finding themselves assimilating on both fronts, a strange distance is created between *them* and *themselves*. It becomes unclear which country to call *home*. This latent condition exists in all of us, and is uprooting the traditional notion of settlement. A new form of homelessness, an *always-on-the-go* lifestyle, will become the norm—perhaps privileging one's speed and frequency of travel, over conventional notions of stability and order.

pp. 30-33 "Satellite House" ©2003 Petar Perisic, Published by 306090, Inc.

Satellite House Conceptual Collage >

UNSTABLE TACTICS OF STATISTICS

IMAGINE YOU ARE AN ELEMENT OF RESEARCH.

Imagine you are an aspect of trivial architecture. Imagine your existence is broken into a spectrum defined by obscure parameters. Imagine you are being morphed through an ever-changing matrix of data. Imagine that you are so non-existent that you are determined by a range of mathematical formulas, extrapolated, and invested with the ability to create chaos out of order. Imagine that the moment you begin to blur you cease to be interesting. Imagine you only live in another's imagination, and only for their purposes.

306090 04 03 | 03

pp. 34–37 "The Unstable Tactics of Statistics" ©2003 Bert De Muynck, Published by 306090, Inc.

It is generally known that architects are poor in explaining their purposes, mainly due to the fact that most of them don't have any.

by Bert De Muynck

Libraries are filled with chaotic literature, analyses of trivial phenomena, future systems and evolutions for non-existing species, information-based architecture, messy volatile rumors, droned visionaries, discussions on never-made-art, and research on unthinkable thinking. It is strange—when we collect, we know we will never have a collection. There are always things missing, changing and shifting through the act of collecting—unless we limit ourselves in that (re)search and put parameters on our existence. Some think that these parameters should be strictly scientific. Some think every collection is the result of a dialectic ideology—the tension between what exists and what one brings together. Research on something as mundane and banal as the collection of socks under one's bed is a good place to begin figuring out existence through ideology or ideology through existence. The intended research is quite easy if one takes existence for granted and has a rigid notion of the seemingly obvious concepts such as socks under the bed.

The moment the barriers between person and space shift, reality is questioned and concepts grow on intellectual grounds. The unstable tactics of statistics brings the everlasting opposition between theoria and praxis into a dialectic and dynamic design happening.

Bert De Muynck is an architect and cultural scientist in Belgium. He received a degree in Civil Engineering in Architecture at the KUL in Leuven. He also holds a certificate in Contemporary Cultural Studies from the VUB in Brussels. His thesis, entitled "The Metamorphosis of the World: Metaphor as a Recipe for Architectural Concept" received the VUB award of High Honours. DeMuynck's biography emphasizes his belief in combining the logic of Andy Warhol and David Bowie: 'They always say that time changes things, but you actually have to change them yourself.' He also states that the most interesting and progressive city in the world is the european capital, Brussels. Nobody believes him.

Contact: bert_demuynck@yahoo.com

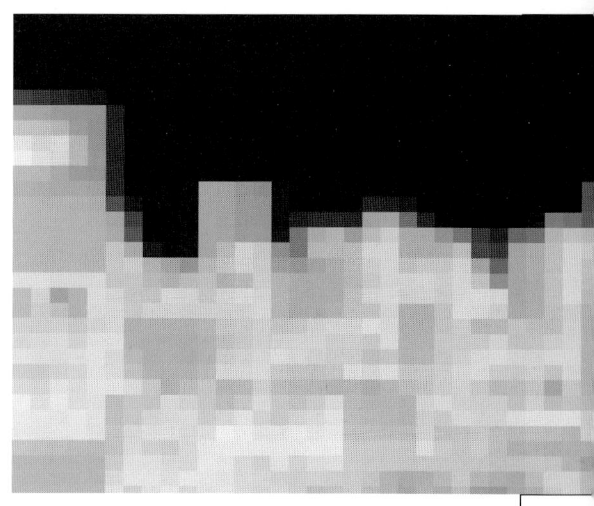

Strange World

Common design uses statistics as a bridge between reality and architecture. For some, this is the only legitimization of its use. Although every new hype follows another, loops another or is a re-mix of an obscure older hype, the bottom line in every discussion remains with the question of what to do with that hype. Did statistics create an architectural catch-22? Is it statistically proven that by using statistics one is statistically better off? Is the added value one attempts to create by using statistics a reason to use statistics?

This world is strange. Information can be overwhelming and weightless. Architects build with porous and holy walls around their designs and stumble theories about point urbanism, inverted metropolitanism, self-reflexive architecture, conscious megalomania and useless symbolism. It is a strange paradox that architects only seem to be able to do this by the suggestion of having a broad view, being beyond solitary thinking, using multi-inspirational sources, using the utmost obscure statistics and by running in the hyper-labyrinth of comatose theories. The medium is no longer the message. The medium became obsolete as soon as it became an idea. Statistics are the opium for the myopic mass.

Metadata and Townships

In the book Metacity/Datatown (1999), MVRDV—a hyped Dutch office—performed research on a city that existed only as data. The exploration of information and statistics was their only tool—"no topography, no representation, no prescribed ideology, no context."[1] After setting these arbitrary parameters MVRDV raises the question: "What is the implication of this city? To what conclusions can it lead?"[2] It is generally known that architects are poor in explaining their purposes, mainly due to the fact that most of them don't have any. MVRDV is an office that attempts to convince others their

purposes are legitimate. But they superficially provoke and then take no responsibility for their conclusions. They play hide and seek in a strange world. It is as if the statistics, data and information are to blame—as if the conclusions of Metacity/Datatown are necessary and are beyond their control, monitored by statistics as divine conclusions. The series of books give the sense that MVRDV's research is based on nothingness. "Datatown is based upon a series of assumptions."[3] Oddly enough, the firm disregards this fact. The Faustian contract made with data takes them far on each discussion.

The maxim for Metacity/Datatown fits on two pages and gives us hallucinating key-words stripped of meaning: "continuous urban fields", "intensify", "world-wide Balkan composition", "emerging agenda" and other hollow, trendy late-nineties sound bytes. The underlying method is simple: "By selecting or connecting data according to hypothetical prescriptions, a world of numbers turns into diagrams."[4] This poly-unstable approach turns illegitimacy into something else. But MVRDV is firm in its method: "Data town, therefore, is not a design; it is not about mix or not-mix, about compositions or relations."[5] This last statement is nicely illustrated with abstract images. The images are so abstract that they must be designed, so independent that they must have a relation, and so seemingly not-designed that they are a reflection of the core topic that they are considering: how to turn not-design into a design that looks like there is no design? Once again one doubts their intentions. This is the only intriguing aspect of their book—the failure of using statistics and information in architecture is nicely illustrated. MVRDV did not try to create a bridge between reality and architecture; they just filled the gap with tons of concrete non-ideas and non-design. Their world is flat, gray, stable, frozen and has no depth whatsoever. Nothing happened, happens and will ever happen. Nothing unexpected will ever emerge. In Metacity/Datatown there is simply nothing out there.

Ideology is conversional thinking

Some say everything is everywhere possible. Those who believe this think themselves to have been freed from a 'prescribed ideology', but are in fact key players in a contemporary ideological game—the ideology of unstable tactics of statistics. Ideology was defined by Daniel Bell as "the conversion of ideas into social levers."[6] For contemporary society this is still valuable. This seems not to be understood by architects because they think having information and statistics equals having ideas. Strangely they are the key-players in that ideology, because they design stability and freeze society that is intrinsically evolutionary. Architects create stability

306090 04 03 | 03

by which people rebel. If they don't rebel, society is dead. If they rebel, architecture is dead. The only future for architecture is a silent take-over and the ideological stimulation of the way information moves and influences statistics.

This ideology—the unstable tactics of statistics—brings together ideas, information and vision in order to supersede both reality and architecture. This goes beyond every concept of creating a bridge. A notion of the unstable condition one designs or works on can justify every action and aim. Every other profession can deal with unstable tactics. If the ideology behind it is strong enough it stays, evolves and interacts with society, if not it disappears and attempts a new form. Concerning architecture, these unstable tactics can allow for one to think there is no ideology in design and everything is possible.

010

The method of acquiring information is binary—you have it or you don't—as information travels and crisscrosses our world. We simply plug in and are overwhelmed by it. In the ideal of MVRDV, no selection of data is necessary, only the neglecting of ideas. The shift they proposed to make has therefore become. MVRDV's unprescribed ideology is the revenge of an ideology that intends no happening, no conversion of ideas. It is simply a fixation—a freezing of society and an extrapolation of weightlessness. I would dare to say that the solidity that melts into the work of MVRDV by research, proposals and abstract designs proves the lack of ideas in using data and information. By existing you understand why it should not exist. Paradoxically it moves and makes people rebel against it. For that should MVRDV be thankful.

IMAGINE YOU ARE DETERMINED BY A RANGE OF MATHEMATICAL FORMULAS, EXTRAPOLATED, AND INVESTED WITH THE ABILITY TO CREATE CHAOS OUT OF ORDER.

Statistics are the leftovers from a party for the ideological society salvation. Architects, who are always one step behind in theory, have to eat them. While the rest of the world ingested ideology, architects only imagined what happened. Architecture is in its worst way the reconstruction of a lost happening, by projecting past statistics on the future.

The unwritten ideology of unstable tactics invites architecture to the table, but does not explain its intentions. This ideology does not invest time and effort in creating for itself an image. And that is where this ideology fails (and wins). It is because of its intrinsic unstable tactic that it is difficult to be taken seriously or respected. On the other hand the affluent design ideology is invisible, taken for granted and superficial. But it is there, and much stronger than before. It lost the rigidity of communism, fascism, capitalism and every kind of other religion. It brought them together and superseded them. That is its strength. And that is the only way it could be represented. People think there is no ideology and that all behavior is appropriate and allowed. It is at that moment that society again interacts in a playful rebellion based on a mutual redefinition of reality and architecture. Architects must participate in this feast. Contemporary design should strive for an idea of constant levering of statistics accordingly to society. Therefore, subtle analysis and unstable projection is necessary—this is the result of ideology.

Unstable Conclusion

The ability to handle mass quantities of information is as ephemeral as the presumption that information has a connection with reality—it doesn't. It has an ideological relation with reality, but not a connection to it. This is performed by the unstable tactics of statistics and expects from the world a critical awareness of dealing with information and statistics. It is out of awareness and relation that one can design and be critical. Either the bridge between reality and architecture should heavily resonate on the edge of collapsing, and therefore to be smartly designed to allow that kind of freedom, or it should be totally invisible and ideologically pointed out in society's mind. The unstable tactics of statistics brings the theoria and praxis of this together in different dialectics and dynamic designs. These bridges only grow by morphing and pushing the edge into the void. In architecture we should design happenings on the edge where data and information can jump in whatever direction, be converted into ideas and be morphed in the quest for a constant social levering.

End Notes:

[1, 2, 3, 4, 5] Winy Maas, 'Datatown/Megacity', 010 Rotterdam, The Netherlands, 1999.

[6] Bell, D., 'The End of Ideology', The Free Press, 1960, p.370.

pp. 34-37 "The Unstable Tactics of Statistics" ©2003 Bert De Muynck, Published by 306090, Inc.

MEGACITY

SHIFTING THE PARADIGM:
Rethinking Global Megacities
Using Dynamic Models

MEGA-CITIES [Cities with 10-Million Inhabitants or More]
Figures are expressed in millions

1975		2001		2015	
Tokyo	19.8	Tokyo	26.5	Tokyo	27.2
New Yurk	15.9	Sao Paulo	18.3	Dhaka	22.8
Shanghai	11.4	Mexico City	18.3	Mumbai	22.6
Mexico City	10.7	New York	16.8	Sao Paulo	21.2
Sao Paulo	10.3	Mumbai	16.5	Delhi	20.9
		LosAngeles	13.3	Mexico City	20.4
		Calcutta	13.3	New York	17.9
		Dhaka	13.2	Jakarta	17.3
		Delhi	13.0	Calcutta	16.7
		Shanghai	12.8	Karachi	16.2
		Buenos Aires	12.1	Lagos	16.0
		Jakarta	11.4	Los Angeles	14.5
		Osaka	11.0	Shanghai	13.6
		Beijing	10.8	BuenosAires	13.2
		RioDeJaneiro	10.8	RioDeJaneiro	11.5
		Karachi	10.4	Cairo	11.5
		Metro Manila	10.1	Istanbul	11.4
				Osaka	11.0
				Tianjin	10.3

[UN World Urban Prospects, 2001 revision]

306090 04 03 | 03

pp. 34-45 "MEGACITY" ©2003 Drura Parrish, Published by 306090, Inc.

by Drura Parrish

The rapid growth of cities has brought about an urban dilemma. Cities are experiencing a radical shift: qualities once take for granted—such as service provisions and economic opportunity—have become nothing more than tragic misconceptions. Traditionally, cities have served as centers of industry and commercial activity. People have flocked to these fiscal islands in search of a better life. New York saw a population explosion in the late 19th and early 20th century as immigrants came across oceans to seek opportunity. Furthermore, London and Manchester harbored millions at the onset of the industrial revolution. These population tides, however, differ from current trends in that a production demand required human bodies to create goods.

The collective perception of an industrial based opportunity lures surging populations to the megacities. Cities are responsible for these perceptions, not its actualization. It becomes responsible for population fluxes through resources, services, and social support. In developing countries, economic support is not yet in place for these new residents. The gap between myth and reality creates a web of psychological and physiological problems that are not easily isolated and addressed.

Drura Parrish graduated with a MArch from the Savannah College of Art and Design after studying Cognitive Psychology at Depaul University. He has been active in the United States and Europe with installations and exhibits through DS Ammar Eloueini, as well as presenting current personal academic interests at conferences. Currently, he is freelancing and devoting his time to setting up "3630", a multi-disciplinary research and design firm.

Contact: drura@3630.net

megacities are becoming too complex to respond with static paradigms

The transition of a city from actuality to ideal (for massive population fluctuations) is diametrically opposed to fixed planning modules and a static model of the city. Important issues in developing megacities are the success of service, and flexibility to meet oscillating needs. Developing countries will have to accommodate up to 184,745 additional urban dwellers daily over the next decade[1]. For each of the new settlers, there is a different set of problems. Traditional models of city planning to isolate problems would be very difficult through macro-planning. Due to this population explosion, contemporary megacities are becoming too complex to respond to how a city ultimately breathes and operates with static paradigms.

In less developed countries, production capabilities have been outpaced by population growth, in turn decreasing capacities to produce and manage services, infrastructure, and shelter; thus further straining the limits of social organization[2]. In this case, major resources are expended for city survival and maintenance, not a better standard of living. Over 800 million inhabitants by the year 2030, twenty percent of the population in the urban areas of developing countries will not be able to provide for shelter, food, water, health, or education[3]. A major shift will have occurred from the role of the city as *producer* to the city attempting survival.

Simultaneously, an environmental toll with proper safeguards is taken. Indoor and outdoor air pollution accounts for 6 million deaths annually, 90% of which occur in developing countries[4]. Water pollution alone accounts for 5 to 12 million deaths per year[5]. Cities account for 80% of all carbon dioxide emissions, as well as 60% of freshwater withdrawal[6]. In this sense, cities are becoming ecological "black holes", drawing upon the resources of entire regions.

Through ecology and commerce, the megacity has the ability to extend influence from individual to city, city to region, region to nation, and nation to world. Large increases in loss from a region tax the country in which they are located. Ultimately, resource depletion affects world operations in the form of pollution, economic instability, and health issues[7]. The megacity becomes part of a larger problem that exits the realm of traditional planning at a global scale—not just one city at a time.

Towards a New Planning Model: Megacity Settlement analogous to U.S. Military Installation Planning

Military bases have been used throughout history to extend authority, acquire wealth and establish outposts. Roman base camps grew into cities, and even monasteries, by utilizing prescribed factors

of Defense. Whether it is through naval yards or air installations, the use is site specific. In contrast to the city as a fixed entity, it can be viewed in the larger context of the globe: the issues affecting a city also affect the world.

The operative word is *extension*. Bases exist as an extension of military service, yet maintain independence. If one is destroyed, other bases do not cease to exist, making it analogous to redundancies within a distributed network. In opposition, centralized cities put all components at risk. If one element is compromised, negative impact can be reverberated throughout the city.

By allowing the city to breathe as a collection of entities, that act in unison, the overbearing fluctuations of population can be better managed by relieving the traditional role of the city as provider. By isolating populations and providing limited autonomy, issues could be located and addressed with ease.

Through re-structuring, ultimate flexibility is achieved. Military planning accounts for a possible population flux of up to 70.8-million persons. This population exceeds the combined population of Tokyo, Bombay, and Mexico City. Although land is scattered across the globe, the possibilities of military planning are enormous.

The Individual

Military base planning utilizes the soldier as its main component of planning. Planning begins with the needs of each individual and potential soldier. Before looking at site, schematics, and other typical planning components, each existing inhabitant of a base, camp, or installation is accounted for as well as the potential flux of new soldiers[13]. It reduces variables into an adjustable element to "plug-in" to the larger picture.

Each soldier needs basic services. As the individual turns to group, and so on, the required service factor increases. These factors are given a required amount of square footage per soldier, and multiplied to ensure service. The output is cross-listed with available private resources in the neighboring city to guarantee expanding needs within the base[14].

Viewing the needs of the city as a whole, this model extends planning to a micro-level—able to be replicated for efficiency and adaptability. The core unit of planning then shifts to individual needs. The variety and level of support is then reviewed for several factors. Most importantly, the evaluation focuses on the maturity of the threat (which refers to the severity and/or time involved in each situation). This affects the actual service units based

to increase trade, protection, and transportation efficiency[8]. In the United States, General James Oglethorpe used the Roman camp model to turn Savannah, Georgia into an overnight installation.[9]

The United States military base and installation structure offers a new planning model for megacities. Currently there are 1.37-million active military personnel. In addition to this population there are 1.28-million on stand-by, as well as 669,000 civilian employees just within the United States Defense structure.[10] The total operating military population can reach 70,819,436 persons through the draft.[11] Furthermore, the existing population of 3.3-million persons on active or stand-by duty are scattered across 519 domestic bases, 61 overseas installations, and 8 territorial installations.[12]

The military acts as a megacity (without the preconceived notion of *city* as a single place)—it exists as a collective entity without bounds. The structure of military installations is flexible and independent, yet it maintains a mutual relationship with the federal government, as the provider of *place*. As a network, the U.S. military exists as clusters of specialized activity globally. Within each of these clusters is a micro-level of planning for individual sustainability and quality of life. These clusters serve as an extension of the Department

306090 04 03 | 03

pp. 34-45 "MEGACITY" ©2003 Drura Parrish, Published by 306090, Inc.

Notes on Megacities

The past 100 years has seen an increased shift of rural populations to urban centers. At the dawn of the twentieth century, 10% of the world's population lived in cities. This number increased to 50% by 2000. Projections show the possibility of over 5 billion city inhabitants in 2030, which will account for 60% of the world's population.[15]

The shift from rural to urban life, plus the natural growth rate in cities, has aided in the creation of the "megacity." Typically, these cities have at least 10 million inhabitants. In 1975, there were only 5 megacities in the world. Today, however, numbers have jumped to 17 and counting. In 2015, the number of megacities is expected to be 21. Additionally, over 564 cities are expected to exceed 1 million inhabitants.[16]

The annual growth rate for developing countries (2.35%) is much higher than that of developed countries (.38%).[17] Many persons in developing countries are inundated with problems that draw them to cities. In countries such as Mexico, deteriorating rural economies have led people to larger centers, such as Mexico City. Wars have led rural villagers in Nigeria to seek harbor in Lagos. Civil unrest has led people to find safety and security in established urban centers. For most of these cities, city sprawl absorbs rural inhabitants.

New populations in some major cities represent the growing majority of city inhabitants. Slum and squatter settlements in some cities are actually as large as or larger than the existing population of the city.[18] These are neither suburbs, nor edge cities; they exist as stepping-stones to harbor new immigrants. They are dependent on the city with little or no reciprocity. The new populations represent "instant cities" themselves, or a base in search of economic opportunity. These instant cities exist as settlements in megacities - they are the temporary harbor for incoming populations. They exist as a sheltering unit, void of most conventions favored by its denizens; such as health and food services, as well as improved public transportation, etc.

306090 04 03 | 03

pp. 34-45 "MEGACITY" ©2003 Drura Parrish, Published by 306090, Inc.

establish a network linking
individual-city-region-nation-world

on that threat. Facilities vary according to troop and unit type. Although the individual is of utmost importance, health, morale, and welfare changes according to the unit type. A unit can be either rotational or permanent; the needs of each are different[19]. Once individual needs are understood, groups can be formed. Settlements can be divided into group needs for ease of planning.

Situational evolution exists in planning and facility construction. Facilities may be more substantial if they are deemed long-term. Generally, military construction begins as temporary construction and evolves if needed. If there is no financial support for resources, the base simply shuts down and distributes personnel elsewhere. In opposition to planned, fixed environments and infrastructure, megacity settlements would benefit by this notion of evolution. As time persists, populations will evolve socio-economically with facilities to accommodate it.

Military installations, however, lack industrial identity. Rather, they represent the shift to a service based economy. The base operates for the maintenance and security of itself, the country, and other bases. This once again points to the autonomous nature of each base, and its symbiotic relationship with other components. The individual is responsible for planning. The planning manifests into a base. The base then serves as the extension of the

Department of Defense, serving as protector and enforcer of United States policy. Purpose is defined by self-service and self-protection. Megacity planning can benefit by subscribing to this support and maintenance model.

City Dependence to National Involvement

Lack of industry in cities should be replaced with a bolstered service based economy. Where no economy exists, an economy must be created. During the Great Depression, FDR championed New Deal. By increasing infrastructure and services, new jobs were created[20]. New jobs eventually turned into prosperity for some. As an offshoot of this domestic plan, new businesses and industries were created resulting in more jobs. By mobilizing and training new immigrants in new trades, it would be possible to create a similar effect. Through socio-economic evolution, instant cities will be able to contribute to their own maintenance and the host city as well.

At the core of military planning, there are very useful tools in engaging urban planning issues in megacities. First, establish a network linking individual-city-region-nation-world. Since city issues have global reach, a policy shift to national levels is of utmost importance. This accommodates a need as methodology shifts from traditional individual-city relationships to match current population trends.

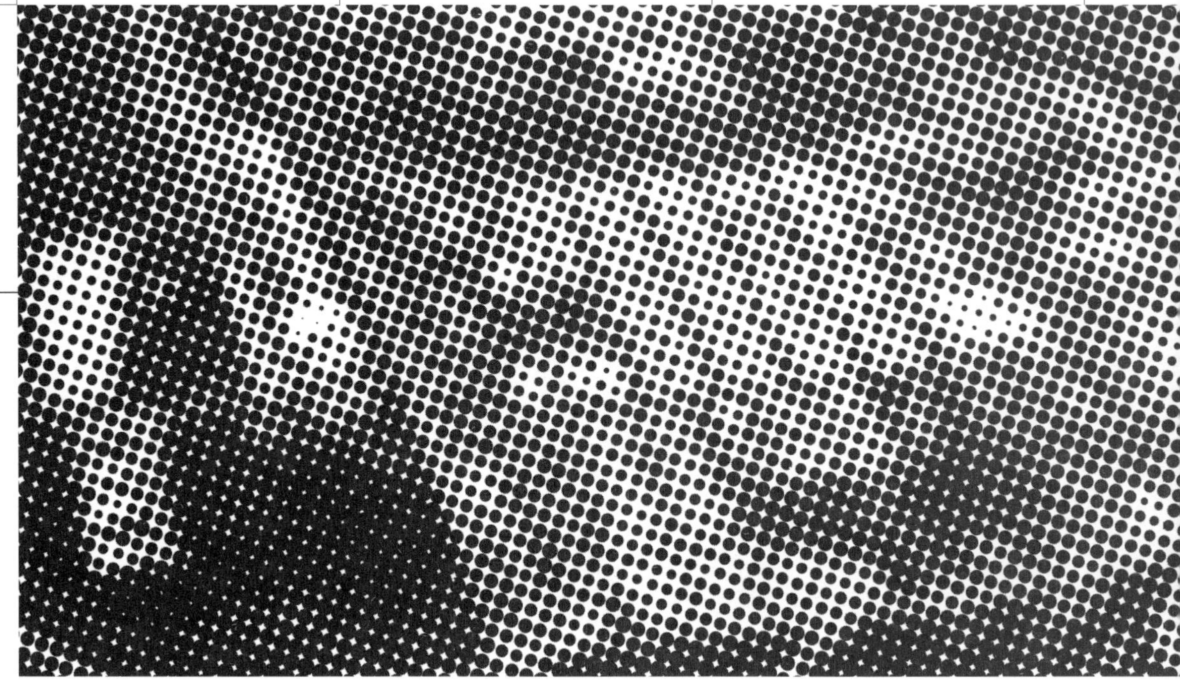

a flexible module which embraces change better addresses these complexities

The national government can serve as financier to settlement needs, but identity will rest on authority within each settlement. This aims to break total dependence on the city, and all possible parasitic characteristics of resource depletion. New settlements should aim at the service mode of military bases. Construction and maintenance should be the employer of the settlement, as well as core city maintenance with other settlements.

Instead of relying on the resources of the city and region for food, agricultural space should be allotted with room to grow per individual. This can occur with land allotment per family with seeds provided by national government. This allows the settlement to become autonomous, relying on the city only for start-up funding and agricultural beginnings. As production exceeds needs, the settlement can service the core city and new settlements.

Educational services should also be provided with training facilities per individual need. The national government will provide start-up costs and maintenance. As the settlement evolves, training facilities will provide for their own educational purposes. The same holds tru for fire, safety, and medical services. As each settlement builds its own foundation, service can be provided to the existing core city and other settlements.

Spatial allocation and construction can also follow military models. The military is responsible for the construction of each base, each with its own construction team. Supplies are provided according to local availability of supplies. With national level involvement, resources can be provided to individuals. This process follows the evolutionary model of the military—building only what is needed. If the plan continues, evolution will guarantee durability. Public areas will receive governmental aid. Recreational areas will be allotted according to individual usage, eventually progressing to public spaces.

Further services such as potable water and roadways will be provided by the government as well. This will include employment of core city laborers to stimulate activity among settlement and host. The policy for environmental management will be provided to ensure quality of resources. As trained individuals increase, environmental services can be provided by settlements.

Current and projected population trends call for a new mode of thought in urban issues. The role of the city has changed as has its inhabitants. Cities are increasingly forced to fight for survival. Burgeoning population needs are drawing resources that are vital to core city existence and profit. Megacities are extending this toll to the world as they place economical, ecological, and social burdens on global support systems. Increasingly cities are becoming inhabitants of the world, and as the world continues to shrink, policy and planning should be revisited to incorporate a belief of mutuality between city, region, country, world and their populations. No longer do cities exist as *islands in the stream*, rather, they are becoming the stream itself. Cities such as Bangkok are expected to account for roughly 10% of the total population of Thailand as well as 80% of its GDP[21]. In such cases the city has metaphorically and economically been transformed to a *city-state*.

Military planning techniques, designed to maintain large populations across vast territories, offers a model for the demographic shifts toward global megacities. Most important is the military's ability to deduce repeatable modules for proliferation. Furthermore, the concept of a flexible module that embraces change better addresses the increasing complexities encountered in megacity planning.

End Notes:

[1] United Nations Population Division p 6.

[2] United Nations Population Fund (UNFPA). State of the World Population 2002: People, Poverty. And Possibilities (New York: UNFPA, 2002) p 16.

[3] UNFPA p 14 with cross reference to United Nations Population Division p 6.

[4] Gardner, R. and Blackburn, R. "People Who Move: New Reproductive Health Focus." Population Reports. Series J, No. 45 (Baltimore: Johns Hopkins School of Public Health, Population Information Program, November 1996) p 28.

[5] Word Health Organization (WHO). Health and the Environment in Sustainable Development-Five Years after the Earth Summit (Geneva: WHO, 1997) p 133.

[6] Rees, W. "Ecological Footprints of the Future." People and the Planet 5(2): 6-9, 1996.

[7] O'Meara, M. Reinventing Cities for People and the Planet (Washington D.C.: Worldwatch Institute, 1999) p 68.

[8] De La Croix, Horst. Military Considerations in City Planning: Fortifications. (New York: George Braziller, Inc., 1972) p 19.

[9] Kristian Hvidt, ed., Von Reck's Voyage: Drawings and Journal of Philipp Georg Friedrich von Reck (Savannah, 1980) 34-35.

[10] Department of Defense Almanac. Active Duty. <http://www.defenselink.mil/pubs/almanac/index.html>.

[11] CIA. The World Fact Book 2002 <http://www.cia.gov/cia/publications/factbook/.>.

[12] Department of Defense. Base Structure Report. (Washington: Office of the Deputy Under Secretary of Defense, 2001).

[13] USAREUR Long-term Base Operations (BASOPS) Strategy for Downrange.

[14] TM 5-803-1 Installation Master Planning. (Headquarters, Department of the Army, 1986) pp 2-11.

[15] National Intelligence Council. Global Trends 2015: A Dialogue about the Future with Non-Government Experts (Langley, Virginia: National Foreign Intelligence Board, Dec. 2000) p 98.

[16,17] United Nations Population Division. World Urbanization Prospects: The 2001 revision (New York, United Nations Population Division 2002) p 77.

[18] United Nations Centre for Human Settlements (HABITAT) Tools and Statistics Unit. Global Trends. <http://www.unchs.org/habrdd/global.html>.

[19] Operation Joint Guard. Base Camp Facilities Standards. (Bosnia, Herzegovina: United States Army, Europe, and Seventh Army, 1997) p 1.

[20] Echeverri-Gent, John. The State and the Poor (Berkeley: University of California Press, 1993) pp39-40.

[21] CIA. The World Factbook, 2002

SASKIA SASSEN
FUTURE-CITIES-LAB
MICHAEL HARDT
REINHOLD MARTIN
DAVID HAYS
NICHOLAS DE MONCHAUX
STEFANO BOERI
KELLER EASTERLING
ATOPIA
MARK JARZOMBEK
NEIL LEACH
STUDENT RESPONSES

from the "Future Cities" seminar instructed by Jason K. Johnson at The University of Virginia School of Architecture

www.faculty.virginia.edu/future-city

Dear XYZ,

As part of the upcoming "Global Trajectories" issue of 306090, we are requesting your assistance. We have drafted two questions engaging this issue's particular subject of exploration. If you choose to reply, your response will be published alongside a series of projects and papers submitted by a group of emerging educators, designers and students from around the world. Your thoughts would be greatly appreciated.

If you have any questions please e-mail us at: editors04@306090.org.

global trajectories e-dialogue

Q1. The UN Population Division projects that 60% of the world's population will live in urban agglomerations by the year 2030. What implications might this have for future patterns of growth, settlement and survival? What are the possibilities? What is the future of cities?

Q2. Network theorists have provided us with powerful tools for the understanding of interconnected organizations. In a world of increasing connectivity, speed, and interdependence, what will be the role of the 'individual' within an increasingly complex network of global cities?

Q1: The UN Population Division projects that 60% of the world's population will live in urban agglomerations by the year 2030. What implications might this have for future patterns of growth, settlement and survival? What are the possibilities? What is the future of cities?

This massive urbanization of the population needs to be deconstructed. It already contains multiple organizational structures: from small fairly isolated towns to deeply networked towns, to megacities, global cities, and vast stretches of built-up territory that has no connection to anything having to do with city-ness. Each of these organizational forms carries specific constraints and possibilities for different social classes, for different types of projects, whether economic, political, environmental, cultural.

SASKIA SASSEN 1/4

Let me just focus on two of these, increasingly widely used terms: megacities and global cities. Both are fundamental building blocks of the urban condition today and in the near future. When we use the term megacities we are referring to size, but size has also come to stand in for severe problems: social, infrastructural and political. In many ways the term is charged with negative meanings, and generally seen as a condition that belongs to the global south. The UN defines megacities as those with 8 million or more inhabitants.

The term global city is a very different concept. A global city is a city that a)has certain types of capabilities—specifically the combination of resources and talent needed to manage and service the global operations of firms and markets, and b) contains, (via its transnational professional class and via the mix of immigrants, asylum seekers, internal minorities) a very inter- or de-nationalized socio-political core. A global city can be large such as London or New York or Paris or Sao Paulo, or it can be small, such as Zurich, or Frankfurt. Size is not the defining feature. However, I hasten to add, that for a variety of reasons, many of the cities that are either global or have global city functions (e.g. Manila, Seoul, Mexico City, Bombay, Bangkok, Shanghai, etc.) tend to be large. Further, there seems to be a threshold effect: very small cities are unlikely to be able to combine the multiple resources to be global or even have global city functions. Thus Zurich and Frankfurt actually operate on a metropolitan scale, where you have the financial functions concentrated downtown but the headquarters of large national and foreign corporations in a broader, even though fairly compact, metropolitan area. Thereby they attain a certain scale of operations and resources.

> Megacities
The driving forces behind megacity growth and global city formation are different. The basic cause for megacity growth is the urbanizing of more and more components of social life, on the one hand, and on the other, the increasing privatizing of (or at least private control over) rural areas. The latter is the crucial factor in the global south: millions and millions of small farmers, tenant farmers, have been forced off the land by the privatization of growing stretches of land by both national and foreign firms. This type of privatization has largely and certainly in the long run created a mass of impoverished migrants who find in the city the last place where they might have a chance at work and survival. There are, however, limits to these growth patterns. Recent UN statistics (World Urbanisation Prospects, the 2001 Revision) suggest that megacity growth has slowed considerably in the 1990s. (e.g. 1970s forecast for Mexico City in the year 2000: 31 million, 2000 census: 18 million;

a similar pattern is evident with Sao Paulo.) This suggests that other organizational forms might emerge in the urbanization of the global south. I think overall there has been a stabilizing and even fall in the numbers, and that it is a result of a mix of dynamics. Underprivileged people are not naive: they understand when they can no longer make a living, when disease and unsafe conditions become overwhelming.

Published by 306090, Inc.

Sao Paulo, Brazil

These megacity growth patterns so present in the global south are not quite evident in
the global north. In the global north we actually have multiple trends, but perhaps the
crucial one is the proliferation of suburbs, exurbs, edge cities and small town living.
Elites, whose size and resources are growing, have tended to move back into the central
cities—and thus been the force behind high income gentrification. But the average
burger probably prefers to live in the outskirts of cities. Urbanites, those with a
deep taste for dense urban living (but it has to be beautiful or at least high class
urban living!) are definitely a minority, even though they are strategic in terms of
the urban landscape—they have inscribed it with their
concepts of lifestyle, their work settings and work
habits.

SASSEN 2/4

I want to return to the issue of thresholds in the
size of cities. There has been a strong tendency to project unilineal growth. Why
were these projections wrong? Some of the numbers reflect actual reversals; some of
the numbers are a function of measurement. How far out are you going to go and still
call it Mexico City? Here are some of the reasons that actually have to do with a
reversal or slow down in growth: Quality of life and work opportunities have declined
sharply over the last decade and a half, really beginning in the 1980s in many of
these cities. Why? Size itself sets limits on job opportunities, on public transport
availability to get to jobs, on housing availability. Secondly, the governments of
these cities have sought to encourage people to go to mid-sized cities in the country
(the Sao Paoulo government, the Mexico City government, all of these have tried, not
very successfully). Thirdly, there has been economic development happening in nodes
outside these large cities that has then encouraged some potential migrants to go
there—though the evidence suggests that this has happened less than might have been
expected. Fourth: underprivileged people actually communicate with each other, they set
up survival systems: for instance, we now know that some urban poor have encouraged
relatives to stay put in the country, produce agricultural goods (food) and then bring
it to market in the city): this has turned out to be a way in which they can use their
kinship groups to enter an interstitial sub-economy in the megacity. They build social
capital that can in turn lead to further "divisions of work" between their urban and
rural based kinship members.

Among the measurement issues: there is the question of where do you set the limit
for the "city;" there is also the fact that over the last 20 years there has been
an increase in extremely poor in-migration and as a result, a growing settlement of
acutely marginal and unsafe areas. These are often not included in censuses; or they
are washed away in mudslides and never counted.

It is important to focus on the question of numbers in all this talk about urbanization
growth. The figures are very problematic. Many of the UN reported figures belong to
very old and poorly executed national censuses. Demographers do not accept some of
these UN figures as very reliable. There are, however, some data sets based on surveys,
that are far better. There is a vast international health indicators data set that
is considered far more reliable. There are also specialized organizations that are
dealing with very particular issues and we have good data on this. For instance, David
Sattherwaite from IEDD—one of the best scholars and activists on much of this—has
focused on, how shall I put it: toilets. Sattherwaite obtained interesting and complex
data on more general conditions—housing, health, public services, clean water access—by
just tracing the toilet/sewage issue. A very different type of effort is my project
for UNESCO—part of a 14 volume new encyclopedia on environmental sustainability,
largely focused on natural science aspects. In my volume on human settlement I set up
a network of over 70 researchers and activists in over 50 countries that produced a
lot of detailed, yes partial, but still detailed information. These partial bits of
information function as indicators of a much broader set of syndromes. Finally, an
effort by the US National Academy of Sciences is of interest here: they decided that it
has become crucial to get data and increase the quality of data about cities because so
much of what constitutes society today happens in cities. They set out an international
panel of experts to develop guidelines for urban data. The hope with this is always
that the US Congress will then support funding, through scientific organizations, to
collect new types of data for cities.

I want to conclude by emphasizing that the problem is not so much the very large city
as such. Cities like Paris, Tokyo and London actually function extremely well. It is
the fact that in so many cases—Sao Paulo, Bombay, Mexico City, Jakarta, and I would
add, to some extent US cities such as New York and Los Angeles—large shares of the

population are abandoned by the political, economic and civic leadership of the city. The ill-health, the extreme poverty, the lack of education for children, the absolute misery of so many children, men and women. There appears to be something unmanageable about a city of 8 million in global south countries, let alone of 18 million. For megacities to function better, something would have to change in both the allocation of resources and the disposition of those with power towards the poor in their cities. De facto megacities have become a problem in social and environmental terms. But as I argue in my introduction to the new Encyclopedia on Sustainable Human Settlement (UNESCO 2003), I think that large cities also offer solutions precisely because of the concentration and hence scale economies that conceivably could be exploited. Cities are part of the environmental problem today but they are also part of the solution..

SASSEN 3/4

> Global Cities
There are in my reading about 40 cities that are either full fledged global cities or cities best described as having global city functions. There is enormous hierarchy in this global network. In the global south, many of the megacities are also global cities. They contain the leading economic and political resources in their countries, they become the gateways for global firms and markets to enter those countries, and also, for those same firms and markets (including some national firms that have gone global) to take national wealth out of the country and circulate it globally. The role and position of these 40 cities in the global system varies: if they are full-fledged global cities they function as key sites for the concentration of resources and capacities crucial to the global economy.

There are also specific subgeographies that connect sets of cities. In the project I just completed, sponsored by the United Nations University, we focused on cities in the global south that are part of this network: Shanghai, Beirut, the Iran-Dubai growth corridor, among others. It is clear that there are emergent global sub-geographies. Sao Paulo articulates a broader southern cone region in Latin America. Dubai and Beirut articulate a middle eastern Arab geography of economic transnationalism. Shanghai has taken over from Taipei as the leading magnet in the region—not just for actual economic transactions but also at the level of the imaginary: there are now 400,000 Taiwanese living in China, mostly in Shanghai. (For details see Global Networks, Linked Cities (Routledge 2002)

These geographies are also strategic and thereby deeply exclusionary. There are multiple reasons for continued growth in global cities at different levels of the global hierarchy. The continued exponential population growth in cities such as Lagos and Dhaka has little to do with global city formation and they are in fact mostly excluded from the new strategic geographies of the global economy. But a similarly large and fast growing city such as Mumbai is a global city, but again, it has little to do with population size.

Sub-Saharan Africa is difficult to understand in this context. Johannesburg clearly fulfills key functions in the global network, functions that no other city in the world can take over, given the diamonds and gold reserves in South Africa. Oil is another vector through which parts of Africa become articulated with very specialized global circuits, but much of the capability for managing the global marketing of oil is not in African cities, nor under the management of African firms. There are very few African cities in the list of 40 that I referred to above.

The increasingly thick and diversified networks that connect cities globally are also networks that can potentially serve political projects, including the projects of the disadvantaged or contestatory.
These can now scale at transnational and even global levels. We might well be seeing the beginning of new micropolitical histories.

Q2: Network theorists have provided us with powerful tools for the understanding of interconnected organizations. In a world of increasing connectivity, speed, and interdependence, what will be the role of the 'individual' within an increasingly complex network of global cities?

< Mumbai, India

I want to answer your second question in terms of the urban condition—a continuation of the first question, and a specific type of individuation—the politics of the disadvantaged in cities.

Is there potential for change? This focus on megacities and global cities of course leaves out much about the future of the urban condition. One wishes that resources and political will were applied to strengthening small towns and village economies which would in principle give most people a better chance at a healthy and reasonable

SASSEN 4/4

life. But national, local and global elites with the resources to do something, seem to have abandoned the 3 billion or more people in the world who are beginning to disappear from the radar screens of the powerful. This is tragic. Then there are another 2 billion who are the laborers in the world who have only one foot left in "history". Why does a world that has such wealth, such enormous administrative capabilities, such scientific capabilities, have to be so grim for over half of its people? How did we get to this point, one where the "utility logics" that organize most of our resources are so narrow, so selfish. The data are overwhelming showing that inequality and wealth concentration have increased sharply over the last twenty years.

In which spheres can we see room for maneuvering, for more equitable and sustainable urban growth? I am often described as an optimist in this, even though I have a hypercritical analysis of globalization. I think there are two kinds of issues. One is that the large concentrations of technical and economic resources represented by global firms could also function as capabilities for solving some of the problems: they could build the infrastructure for water and transport, the housing, that are so desperately needed. Oil and mining companies could decide to use environmentally friendly technologies of extraction and production. The US is rich enough to provide vast amounts of dollars for particular needs and to redeploy its doctors and lawyers for good causes around the world. (Even when I think of the 200 billion the bombing of Iraq (we can hardly call that a war) could cost: imagine putting it into health care services in a few poor countries!

Does the vast financial and economic crisis, the impending environmental disasters at some point cross a threshold in the minds of the top political and economic decision-makers and does it lead to a concerted effort towards global survival? When you see one global, supposedly invincible firm break down, does it signal that something is not going right, does it open the mind of those with power to alternative possibilities?

The second issue is the potential of politics to bring about change, even when it is the politics of the disadvantaged, of those who lack power. I do believe that politics is a bridge to a better world. By politics I mean that people, the multitudes are potentially political actors that can make a difference. If you look at our history you see that no formal system of power has lasted for ever, and even more importantly, that these systems have mostly been brought down by their own abuses of power by what appeared as "disorganized" masses. I think there are multiple micropolitical forces and architectures taking shape in the "multitude."

I use the term multitude in quotations because I think it is a somewhat uncritical category: it suggests the masses out there. I am trying to say that the "masses" are at least partly constituted in terms of political projects and architectures. These may be micro-projects and micro-architectures, invisible to power or to the middle classes. But they are there. I think that the emergence of experiences of globality, of being interconnected, of the recurrence of certain struggles in community after community around the world, can feed a sense of politics and of viable struggles. However, the fight is against an enormously powerful mix of financial, technical, and ideological resources. And the fight can only succeed, perhaps, if power becomes so powerful that it abuses its own power. I would say, we are almost there.

> Saskia Sassen is the Ralph Lewis Professor of Sociology at the University of Chicago, and Centennial Visiting Professor at the London School of Economics.

Her most recent books are Guests and Aliens (New Press 1999) and the edited Global Networks, Linked Cities (New York and London: Routledge 2002). The Global City is out in a new fully updated edition in 2001. She has also just completed for UNESCO a five-year project on sustainable human settlement for which she set up a network of researchers and activists in over 50 countries. Her books are translated into fourteen languages. She serves on several editorial boards and is an advisor to several international bodies. She is a Member of the National Academy of Sciences Panel on Cities, a Member of the Council on Foreign Relations, and Chair of the new Information Technology, International Cooperation and Global Security Committee of the Social Science Research Council (USA).

 The idea of the 'urban agglomeration' is something that initially implies an inherent decentralization—a sprawling system operating in a seemingly homogenized vacuum. The agglomeration of urban densities however, might be explored as a set of interrelated networks of varying dimensions, intensities, and scales. The global network is one thing, the network of individuals is another, and the molecular structures of human life are yet another—and these are only three scales. We do not read the future as a uniform tarp of continual information and homogeneity. On the contrary, the cities of the future will be dynamic bundles of interrelated multi-scalar networks of energy, creativity and capital. The potential result is profound, and yet there are serious obstacles.

FUTURE-CITIES-LAB.net 1/1

The ramifications of rapid population growth in the next millennium are well documented: resource depletion, environmental ruin, disease, famine, social conflicts and warfare. A 15 year-old boy growing up in central Africa has a 90% chance of dying of AIDS/HIV. In October of 1999, the six-billionth child was born. Extrapolating forward, we must ask the question: how are we going to house, feed and care for the 10 billion people that are going to be living on the planet in the next century? These are issues that are not going to disappear any time soon. They will require fundamental social, political and cultural foresight, along with infrastructure change in order to allow us to move forward in a positive way.

Nevertheless, certain issues that are fundamental to thriving urban environments can offer us optimistic visions for the future: interconnectivity, interdependence and density. The impact these may have on our understanding of global agglomerations is not one of fear for lack of diversity and homogenization, as much as a search for multiple threads of intimacy, alternative modes of interconnectedness and optimism for what will inevitably emerge.

The role of the individual is coupled with the notion of convergence. The global city and the interconnectedness of our world make the potential impact of the individual on a system much greater and more powerful. The individual is capable of triggering a ripple through the network resulting in a wave of dynamic "reoccurrence" and "repercussion".

The potential for the individual to remain anonymous and be engulfed in a homogenized network of operation is a danger that implies the need for initiative and independence. It is in the freedom of the individual that the possibility for diversity exists. In a surprisingly sociopolitical manner, the individual has gained power to affect and be affected, to alter the global system and receive its impact, to live in a diverse field of exchange, or in voluntary isolation. The individual has the choice. The results are nonetheless always global.

> FUTURE-CITIES-LAB is an interdisciplinary research collaborative directed by Jason Johnson and Nataly Gattegno. Both partners are currently teaching design studios and research seminars in computing, urbanism and information theory at the University of Virginia.

Web: www.future-cities-lab.net

Mexico City

Q1: The declining distinction in today's global landscape between the country and the city has enormous political consequences. One characteristic that used to define rural populations, such as peasants, and restrict their political capacities was their lack of communication and cooperation. The reason that socialist and Marxist traditions have almost all given priority to the urban working class over the rural is the possibility (and even necessity) of communication in urban life in general and particularly in the factory. Rural populations, in contrast, were seen as isolated and outside of communication. This gave rise to the view that the peasantry should subordinate itself to the lead of the urban proletariat, which would act in its interest—a view that gave rise to numerous disasters.

MICHAEL HARDT 1/1

In any case, today, networks of communication and cooperation can potentially extend all across the globe and throughout each society. This does not mean that we all have equal access to communication, but that we could. The possibility of a communicating and cooperating global society appears on the horizon as a potential political project.

Q2: The individual may be a concept in the process of extinction. I don't mean that we are all becoming the same, that we are melding into one indifferent mass— on the contrary. I mean rather that our differences may no longer be defined by our individuality. The concept of the individual may not be able to grasp all the multiplicities that are emerging! We are becoming partial and collective subjectivities that extend above and below the level that traditionally defines the individual. The constellation of these differences and these multiplicities that cooperate and function in common in society might be given the name multitude.

> Michael Hardt is Associate Professor of Literature and Romance Studies at Duke University. He is author of *Gilles Deleuze: An Apprenticeship in Philosophy* (1993) and coauthor with Antonio Negri of *Labor of Dionysus: A Critique of the State-form* (1994) and *Empire* (Harvard, 2000). He is coeditor with Paolo Virno of *Radical Thought in Italy* (1996) and coeditor with Kathi Weeks of *The Jameson Reader* (2000).

Bess Wellborn: The language of walking and communication as we have known it—without the speed of interconnectivity—will be lost and as such, the language of the city may turn to that of a totally different scale, type, and time. Yet because the fragility and resiliency of the environment is still unknown, it is uncertain just how such a mass of people and networks can sustain its own environment (land value, quality, biodiversity, etc.) without total debilitation or destruction.

As the individual gains greater momentum in terms of power, ability to simulate, control, and monitor emergence, the individual will subvert the established hierarchical system and begin shifting relations in both the physical and political realms. The individual may redefine

STUDENT THOUGHTS 1/3

scales of geographic systems, redefine the networks of the environment and consequently live within new boundaries of political, social order, space, and time.

> Bess Wellborn, Graduate Student at the School of Architecture, University of Virginia

Nathan Petty: In a world that is exploding in population, how does one keep their own identity? Perhaps it is the products that we use that will ultimately define us all. We are all consumers. Nevertheless, people must be able to differentiate themselves from the thirty other people in the Metro car next to them. Ease and effectiveness of choice is vital to the survival of our identity, both at the scale of the individual and the urban agglomeration. The web of infrastructure will not outdate itself. It's only their constituent products that will outdate themselves and need to be replenished. The "Delux Mag-lev" will ultimately replace the first "Mag-Lev," and so on and so forth...

> Nathan Petty, Undergraduate Architecture Student at the University of Virginia

Q1: To be honest, I'm more concerned about 2003 than 2030. Survival of what? Of whom? Sounds like homeland defense to me (the UN source notwithstanding). Especially because certain assumptions are easily overlooked in that tradition in urban ecology that thinks of cities and populations as ecosystems following patterns of growth mapped by statistics. Since what the statistics tend to repress is the politics of numbers.

Another way of thinking about this is through ecology's etymological relative, economy. The two words share the same root: oikos, or home. Ecology: the logic of the home. Economy: the law of the home. The nineteenth century gave us political economy as a way of analyzing the forms of domination associated with certain sets of numbers, like profit. But the twentieth century failed, by and large, to give us a political ecology. And so we are left only with numbers that say this or that will happen, and techniques like risk analysis that determine the odds of survival and the statistical necessity of preemptive action. Which is to say that ecology always winds up projecting a defense of the home. Another name for this is urbanism. It always has been and, unfortunately, always will be.

What are the alternatives? Watch television. There you'll see the logic of homeland defense (ecology, or duct tape) and the law of homeland defense (economics, or oil) at work. And how about some statistics on the destabilizing effects in Nigeria (including Lagos) of increased American speculation on oil sources outside the Middle East? Finally: Never naturalize.

Regarding the future, architects might begin by realizing that—like ecologists manipulating population curves and economists manipulating dollar signs—they too manipulate politically active symbols. That would be a start. Since ultimately the future is radically speculative, in exactly the same sense that numerical speculation on oil futures has been feverish with the promise of war, or homeland defense.

Q2: There is no opposition between the individual (consumer) and the network. The consumer obsessed with their own individuality is the engine that drives the global network. Such a consumer may even be the first product of globalization, rather than its first victim. By extension, there is no opposition between isolated objects like consumer products or buildings and networks (ABC, CBS, NBC, Fox, CNN). Each requires the other.

This is especially true at the level of design. Think of the cell phone, where the fetishistic articulation of the physical object as a "wireless" (i.e. disconnected, liberated) token of economic status, social autonomy, and personal style is a function of that object's actual connectivity within a network. In other words, the more symbolically and physically individualized a cell phone gets, the more it belongs to a larger physical and symbolic system, field, or network. Similarly, the first thing that is "organized" in and by such networks is an individual's "personal identity," in the form of passwords, data mining, and racial profiling. The anonymity of the crowd is a thing of the past. We must seek our alienation elsewhere.

So the first victim of such processes is anyone who does not qualify as a consumer, and thereby cannot gain access to the network in the first place. This is one sense in which the refugee has replaced the stranger as the archetypal figure of (post)urban isolation.

The individual (read: consumer) is the engine that drives the network. S/he is an instrument and effect of power. Call this The iMac Principle (Think different).

Q1: Cities depend on their "surroundings," and much will be determined by how those territories are reconceived and renegotiated in the decades ahead. As new imperatives unfold and domains are transformed, perhaps the most telling—and daunting—picture of our collective urbanism will be the shifting geography of all that lies beyond it: the redundant, the uncontested, the overlooked, the unnegotiable.

Q2: Should the "world of increasing connectivity, speed, and interdependence" – which is not the world—become the world, then—as in war—the individual will surely be everything and nothing.

DAVID HAYS 1/1

> David L. Hays is currently an Assistant Professor in the Department of Landscape Architecture at the University of Illinois Urbana-Champaign. He holds a BA (Fine Arts and Romance Languages and Literatures), Harvard University; MArch, Princeton University; PhD (History of Art), Yale University.

Amy Lewandowski: People gather. Even in primitive cultures one sees the human tendency to form groups that work together to achieve outcomes far superior to the capabilities of a single individual. This instinctive grouping of individuals has lead to the development of mega-agglomerations (cities that continue to grow and develop with no end in sight). In the very near future, it is predicted that 60% of the world's population will reside in urban areas. This means that most individuals will be collected with specific global zones—working and interacting with one another. What happens when these "nodes" continue to grow? The cities and their masses, growing outward and outward, will expand until they begin to overlap and merge to form even larger agglomerations.

As these nodes grow outward we are forced to face the reality that they might not expand in a typical fashion and must look to new dimensions for expansion. For example, the island of Japan is bounded on all sides by water and will one-day reach a point where the limit must be redefined. This is already evident in the city of Tokyo where the maximization of space is crucial. The city grows in the vertical dimension out of necessity. Each space must be compressed and maximized. No doubt, as the city and country grows in population and scale, even its water boundaries will become elastic.

> Amy Lewandowski, Undergraduate Architecture Student at the University of Virginia

STUDENT THOUGHTS 2/3

Michael Krop: As resources run out and diseases spread, our natural tendency to consume could control the future of our cities. Steven Johnson's observations on slime molds offer startling insight into the possible future of urban growth: "I see them [slime molds] on the screen, growing and dividing and I think: that way lies the future." [1] Boundaries are fluid now—one could move to different cities, but never know it. Los Angeles is a classic example. One hundred and twenty-five towns fill the Los Angeles basin—many of which are now just neighborhoods in an ever-expanding city. Even with the absorption of more and more people into the agglomeration, the life of the individual amongst the whole will not be lost. Johnson observes that the slime mold fluidly "… oscillates between being a single creature and a swarm." [2]

Notes: [1,2] Steven Johnson, "Emergence" (Scribner, NY, 2001)

> Michael Krop, Undergraduate Architecture Student at the University of Virginia

Q1: If you found yourself chatting to an inhabitant of the Iberian Peninsula in 500 AD, a Bavarian lowlander in 900 AD, an inhabitant of the Tatra mountains in 1400 AD, and asked each of them to describe their identity, their answers might surprise you. Instead of answering as you might expect (a Spaniard, a German, a Balkan), each of them would tell you—proudly—that they were a 'Roman.'

Surprised? Thanks especially to Victorian historians and their contemporary preoccupations (no rise without fall, after all), we are used to thinking of 'Rome' as having ended at one of a collection of administrative or military markers (see second answer, below). Yet these markers are as arbitrary as the numbers that describe their dates. If we listen instead to the self-proclaimed identity of our historical companions, and their pride in a shared, significant cultural inheritance, we can learn a great deal about the nature of cities in the past, and the future.

The story of an increased number of human beings moving towards cities is not so much a story of numbers, as much as it is a story of aspiration, achievement and identity. In the past 150 years, for example, the cities of this country have served, nationally and globally, as magnets for the aspiration of the disenfranchised, refuges for refugees. Cities, with their senses of order and opportunity represent both a venue for rapid movement between ideas, and the venue for renewing, defining, and changing identity.

And what is identity? If we look at the word itself, from the Latin (Roman), idem et idem, we find it means not a fixed quality, but literally "again and again," that which is shared, across space, and time. We move to cities to share their qualities—change, speed, possibility—but also to gain a sense of belonging from our very participation in that change.

Our cities, then, are a common space in time—past, present, and future. Of the cities of 2030, it is most important to say the following:

The new population of cities represent a continuing, and important shift, and should be understood most important group of citizens (from the French citean, from the Latin/roman civitas, of a city) the world will be presented with in the coming decades. How will we welcome these new citizens, be they Muslim, Christian, "black," or "white?" How will we allow our cities, our shared identity, to change and adapt to accommodate them? (We can already see that some potential adaptations—from heightened cultural tolerance to the sharing of limited resources—water, oil, information—seem barely within our grasp).

Depending on the answers to these questions, the cities of 2030 will represent new possibilities of acceptance, cultural hybridization, and political and economic opportunity—or, they will represent new and unexpected mutations of intolerance, terror, and violence. What our cities, our identities, will become, is—like any complex process—unexpectedly subject to each of our future actions. But wherever we find ourselves in 2030, we will dwell in the ideal, and reality, of the city.

Q2: When German forces crossed the Danube in 69 AD, the news reached Rome within 25 minutes, via a networked chain of signal fires whose illumination was pre-agreed to signify a frontier attack. After the signal reached Rome, specific instructions to military posts were dispatched through a network of fast horses, along a system of straight and swift paved roads, within 24 hours.

Instead of attempting to understand the effects of information change on the nature of "cities," we might better understand the "city" itself to be an object defined by information and its exchange. From this perspective, cities can be understood to have appeared as a pre-industrial technology for those sustaining events elaborated by current network theorists and students of complex systems—adjacency, opportunity, and the exchange of information. Without a reasonable number of these events, it is asserted, any self-sustaining system, organization or organism, will fail to survive. Through increased physical and temporal proximity, cities and their surprisingly stable

DE MONCHAUX 2/2

tropes—the agora, the theater, the busy street—rapidly improved the physical and temporal scale at which these sustaining events could take place in human societies and systems.

In speaking of the health of a complex system (its ability to sustain itself and grow), a contemporary network theorist—biologist, chemist, or economist—would describe a crucial balance. The structure of a healthy system—of molecules, people, or information—must include a structured basis for adjacency, opportunity, or exchange, but not be too structured. This factor—the 'messiness' of a system, can easily be translated to cities as we know them, and their sometimes tragic vulnerability to over-structuring or over-anticipation (highways, slum clearance, 'planned' communities). Our new cities will have to struggle to maintain the equality of access, to resources and opportunities, that have accompanied their historic success.

In trying to understand the future of cities, then, I would point to a crucial opportunity; not to attempt to redefine cities relative to current changes in our ability to exchange and process information (electronically, chemically, biologically), but rather, to enlarge our definition of cities based on new understandings of information processes.

What then, is a city? And what might we gain from expanding our sense of the urban to include not just a picture-book set of skyscrapers, but, rather, any body that sustains our selves and our culture through the medium of information exchange? Are we as physical bodies not ourselves cities, with our own informational structure (our genes and senses), and physical needs, subject to as much ambiguity, and possibility as our developing urban future? And might it be wrong to draw a distinction between the two?

An important benefit of such a perspective might be not only a new the understanding of the city in space, (the 'redevelopment' of a strand of DNA, the 'infill' opportunities of a global network), but the re-evaluation of the city in time. One of the earliest arti-facts of urban culture is a sense of tolerance and obligation towards one's neighbors—but we all too easily forget that these neighbors lie in the past and future, as well as the present.

> Nicholas De Monchaux is an Assistant Professor at The University of Virginia. He received his MArch from Princeton University. Recently he received awards from the International Union of Architects and the 2002 Pamphlet Architecture Competition. He was the recipient of the 2000 John Dinkeloo memorial fellowship of the Van Alen Institute, and is a member of the Society of Fellows of the American Academy in Rome. In the Spring of 2003, he was a visiting scholar at the Santa Fe Institute. His book, "Spacesuit: 21 Essays on Technology, Complexity, and Design" is forthcoming.

Q1: The gradual blurring of the notion of "city" as a principle of spatial and social order. The proliferation of superficial descriptions enphatizing the chaotic nature of urban settlements. The necessity of a substantial renovation of our theoretical paradigms.

[What are the possibilities?] "City" doesn't exist any more. But "Cities"—as individual configurations multiplied in the contemporary space, within huge urban settlements—shall continue to live and growth. We should learn to recognize the new, invisible, local rules which are hidden behind any individual urban configuration and which are contributing to distinguish it.

STEFANO BOERI 1/1

[What is the future of cities?] As always, there isn't "one" future. A multitude of cities means a multitude of possible, unpredictable trajectories.

Q2: Some recent social commentary has identified an apparent and pervasive "fluidity" in social and cultural relations found in modern society—especially in Europe—and gives the view of a "smooth" geopolitical map. In this map, the social substrata and the hierarchical super-structure is reduced and the individual takes its place over and above the whole social organization. Many of these views on the importance of population flows in the contemporary world are verified by studies in architecture, town planning and geography. Although these different, but at the end convergent, interpretations are symbolically persuasive in their message of the 'flow' in the contemporary world, they tend to observe the movements that have been deemed media-worthy and are in the public eye.

A careful study of our surroundings shows us a contrasting phenomenon. Wherever one looks at living spaces today, they in fact offer a proliferation of borders, walls, fences, thresholds, signposted areas, security systems and checkpoints, virtual frontiers, specialized zones, protected areas and areas under control. The multiplication of fences and sub-system controls (which in the contemporary world take on many different, and often, changing appearances) is an inevitable—if not surprising—outcome of any study and mapping of territory.

As much as this proliferation of walls and borders can and should be seen as the result of the pervasive population flow, their heterogeneous and especially micro nature, show us that the two processes are not simply opposing or complimentary. Population flows and confinements are not two extremes of the same process of a territory's economic and social adaptation; they are not the opposites of an evolutionary phase in our society.

From a study of the infinite restrictions that space places on an uncontrolled flow of population into a particular territory, and the social relations that follow it, a kaleidoscope of boundary devices can be called up that has nothing to do with the mirroring of geographical fluctuations in population or even with the traditional subdividing of the modern map in large political, social and cultural areas.

A careful study of geographical boundaries that gives a different representation of the world and our societies could read the proliferation of fences and sign-posted areas (both the controversial as well as the ordinary ones) as a reflection of the many highly charged instances of identity and protection that explode everyday between groups in our multi-faceted societies.

This could reveal the densely differentiated and kaleidoscopic nature of our contemporary societies. And our local territories, our local "Cities"-within this hypothesis-can be interpreted as important metaphors for the whole of society.

> Stefano Boeri is an architect based in Milan. He is architectural consultant to the Triennale and has had articles published in countless magazines in and out of Italy. He was guest lecturer at the Berlage Institute in Amsterdam and is presently professor at the Universities of Milan and Genoa.

Q1: "Parks" (orgman patois for enclaves) are strange warm pools of global urbanism. They are the units of agglomeration in the large conurbations surrounding inland or ocean-going ports, airports and the manufacturing zones. Their program cocktails include logistics centers, IT campuses, export processing zones, offices and calling centers are global contagions. If the global city as financial center is organized vertically by the elevator, the global city as logistics center is organized horizontally by automated devices that continually convey and sort material from container transshipment in parks.

KELLER EASTERLING 1/2

While parks may accrete at the periphery of cities like Hong Kong, they are not anything like suburbs that domesticate and flatten the urban excesses. Often free trade zones, they are global exurban formations that imbricate the presence of other countries within the host country. Park infrastructure is also often tied, not to the local grid, but to a global grid or satellite broadcast. Park is, consequently, not sited by locality but rather positioned within a global network of similar enclaves. It may surround a large metropolitan area or benefit by some degree of isolation, locating a temporal distance between metropolitan areas. Some global companies develop similar parks all around the world with a peculiar form of sovereignty that brings to mind the mercantile companies of another time. American cities owned by Finland. Dutch cities owned by China. Chinese cities owned Germany. All sheltering functions and secrets in Dubai. Just like the old days.

Parks avoid laws and politics related to locality, streamlining customs and labor processes, even trading on these loopholes and benefits transnationally to, for instance, launder the identity of a product or utilize inexpensive labor. They often run on a platform of optimized logic. Yet, although a space of exemption, as they become pawns in regional rivalries, these SEZs ironically land in the cross hairs of political and territorial conflicts. Many of these new logistics conurbations develop in archipelagic formations that are already fraught territorial disputes and haunted by piracy, terrorism, refugees, tax sheltering, labor migrations and labor exploitation . They are always about to implode and always about the encounter error, information and urbanism, even when they try to grow and colonize in the absence of information.

Globalization theorists sometimes like to imagine one civilized ecumenical world threatened by tribal fanaticism. It must be easy for them to distinguish between believers, to tell the difference between religious fanaticism and logical fanaticism, for instance, or to distinguish between what is primitive and sophisticated or to identify something that looks like democracy. Cities that multiply their enemies and believers, amassing circumstance and error, are often beautifully resilient, but might it be a myopic spell that induces the belief that familiar forms of urban intricacy represent an evolved state? Perhaps there is no evolution in the warm pool. Cities of every scale and type become attractive targets of righteous aggression that would deny the information and complexity that seems to draw our faith. And yet, cities of every scale and type are also ready to deal the blow. If it is not a myopic spell, perhaps there is future for cities, in making their intelligence, and their non-national status instrumental in preventing the aggression.

Q2: From audio recordings played in the car or the jet, the markets overhear the network theories of management gurus and globalization pundits adopting complexity scripts. In popularizations of network, theories of multiplicity sometimes mysteriously yield theories of monism, sending a silent call to all believers, reactivating sonorous philosophical catachisms, cybernetic dreams of network, and existing geometric fascinations of architects. This is the dream of one world, a soft world, a single domain of connectivity that constantly, but only gently, learns and adjusts, providing the illusion of differentiation in the network. It is a world where catastrophes errors or negations are, like Satan, part of the family of the whole, and "the" individual is something like drop of water in globalization's many maritime metaphors.

The market likes this word soft, incorporating it into the argot and the logo of its world, its fictional arena of agglomerating expertise. Not just a career costume for the academic, network theory is part of an elaborate set of vestments and disguises useful in keeping the bloated power of a world intact and undetected. From segregated enclaves, "parks" with seccessionary infrastructure on the ground and in the air, markets speaks magnanimously of soft, of one world of feminized synergistic organization, sprinkled with Kevin-Kellyesque aphorisms. They are believers too, in one world, one domain that competes with and forces compatibility from other worlds. The loop preserves and shelters information, eradicating error, and denying contradictory extrinsic information. They are working hard to keep individuals connected. Its the perfect masquerade when exploiting global sources of cheap labor, previously the classic individual, the classic subject to be considered in a population.

Resisters to these neoliberal masquerade, to individuals "riding the wave," are also often believers, equally perfect, monistic and intact. The left's perfectly tragic counter-culture regards the individual worker as the citizen of an oxymoronic authentic locality, and the only righteous tool of negation.

EASTERLING 2/2

Empire, while departing from this perfection, also flirts with monism. The individual is part of a "plural multitude that has learned to sail this sea," and yet, the individual is also at once Empire and counter-Empire, able to use any and all of the same tools to redirect and resist. It is a spongy organizational paradigm, at once monolithic and porous to the individual, in a way that collapses the difference between tactic and strategy.

Somewhere here, where negation and network is not a singular, but distributed and multiplied, is an opening for the individual as non-believer, a non-believer operating in a plural condition where the segregated logics of worlds collide. This is error. Error is information, and information is network. Networks are only everything else, everything within which they are embedded, and when embedded in political territories, would never provide obedient demonstrations of connectedness and synergistic feedback. Familiar theories of immanence in multiplicity might just as easily inspire another character who cannot exist in a monistic world or a homogenous sea. This individual is not a hacker, part aboriginal part omniscient cyborg of an totemic global village. This individual is probably not a Bartleby, either, the savior and hero of entrenched passive resistance, who also remains violently intact. Perhaps this individual is closer to a pirate, a non-believer, a roaming sinner who, given the chance, would never dream of maintaining one domain, but would, rather, engineer a life of responsibility and corruption using many masks and disguises to translate between worlds, to make and harvest error, to keep many domains alive.

> Keller Easterling is an architect, author and Associate Professor at Yale University. She received her MArch degree from Princeton University. Her recent book, Organization Space: Landscapes, Highways and Houses in America (MIT Press 1999), applies network intelligence to a discussion of American infrastructure and development formats. She is currently working on a book titled, Terra Incognita about spatial products in pivotal political locations around the world.

Q1,Q2: The trajectory of global urbanization since 1944 and critically since the mid 1970s, from Bretton Woods to the Battle of Seattle and beyond, suggests that a radical re-localization of production, and a redefinition of regional and local categories of territory will be seen, indeed may be in evidence already.

The conflicting pressures on urban areas that simultaneously force centrality and dispersal, entropic diffusion and centripetal accumulation, render useless any

ATOPIA 1/1

catalogue of types that might have been deployed in a restorative capacity, break apart the reductive clichés of the neighborhood, district, street, park, garden or square, dismantle pre-existing distinctions between the center and the periphery, and demand an assessment of the interdependent effects and impact of economic globalization, ecological crisis and electronic communication on urban form. The opportunities for architecture as a discipline are immense, but insist upon the immediate recognition that tools are merely tools, that what buildings do is more important than what they look like, and that cities will never match the dream-images of any generation. They are what they are, and there is work to be done.

Individuality remains central the notion of creativity, to the making of an innovation milieu, to discourse. Work would be worthless without creative individuality.

The lesson of Seattle, and of the recent anti-war demonstrations in cities around the world, is the countless examples of individual and collective action made easier by the catalytic instrumentality of knowledge networks—the intimate exchange of ideas, close-up or at a distance—are that however attenuated the mind, body, environment continuum may become, individuality is not at risk.

> Jane Harrison & David Turnbull - ATOPIA, USA & UK

Jane Harrison is currently a Lecturer at Princeton University School of Architecture and the Cooper Union. David Turnbull is currently a Professor of Architecture at the University of Bath, England. They are currently collaborating on a book entitled, *Fast Cities: The Accelerated Space of Advanced Capitalism*, (Academy Editions, forthcoming).

Georgianna Salz: Generally, humans lead themselves quite well. Individuals work to survive—whether in the "first-world" model where economic prosperity usually equals survival, or the "third-world" model of people simply surviving. While the

STUDENT THOUGHTS 3/3

first-world is very comfortable, its expansion and prosperity comes at the cost of the environment and the less privileged. The current state will continue as long as it is the social norm. Our social and work habits will continue the physical growth of the agglomerations, even as city populations remain almost static.

For most individuals, world connectivity will not matter. For others it brings a sense of "disconnect" [living far from home, yet being able to read about the weather + politics + communicating with people at a distance]. The network of cities + connectivity + speed [etc.] might not be so complex. The implications of passing stuff [the metaphoric Cyclic AMP] between individuals far away from each other might have implications and create global movements of individuals. The actual role of the individual might not change, but the nature of the group movement may—the global community, instead of local community. We may re-define the meaning of the word "local" to mean closeness in terms of "social/cultural/political" terms instead of physical locality. Place and location will become more ephemeral and defined by relationships to other people, rather than physicality.

> Georgianna Salz, Graduate Architecture Student at the University of Virginia

in favor of the pragmatics of "sustainable development." For better or worse, the new
breed of Environmental Managers is soon to take over that agenda. The question, "What is
the future of cities?"—is hopefully still a philosophical issue, which brings me to the
movie, "Dark City." [1998], directed by Alex Proyas. It has more to say about the "future" of cities than most urban planners. As that film suggests even in 23rd century,
even under the rule of an alien species, the city is a place where symbolic and narra-
tive power coalesce with par-
ticular poignancy. The hero's
struggle to leave the city, to
see it on the horizon from the
beach, turns out, in the end,
to be possible only once he has
himself mastered the urban fiction.

MARK JARZOMBEK 1/1

Q2: The second question is very abstract, especially since the concept "the
individual," these days, seems a bit old-fashioned. We can no longer talk about "the
individual" except as a function of some larger corporate principle, whether that
is religion, nation, work, play and capital. In other words, it was once possible
to see The Corporation and The Individual as antithetical. But in the last fifty
years, organizational systems have attacked all aspects of The Individual. Maybe our
connectivity is such that we have come to be bound to each other in ways that are
positive and that can indeed contribute to an improved life for all, but I suspect
that a lot of our "connectivity" is an excuse to connect with some and disconnect with
others. In other words, we may live in a world in which technology has made certain
type of connectivity possible, but that does not solve—or alter—the fundamental problem
of human nature.

> Mark Jarzombek is an Associate Professor at MIT. He is currently Director of the History Theory Criticism Section
in the Department of Architecture. He is a historian of modern and Renaissance architectural history and aesthetic
theory. He has published a book on the aesthetic theory of the Renaissance intellectual, Leon Battista Alberti, and
numerous articles on twentieth century subjects.

NEIL LEACH 1/1

Q1: Rumors of the death of the city, which persisted until very recently, were clearly exaggerated. There are various points of urban intensity—metropolitan "hot-spots"—that are proving ever more popular. Yet while some urban agglomerations—such as Shanghai—are mushrooming at a remarkable rate, others—such as some cities in the former GDR—are shrinking. The prediction of patterns of urban expansion and contraction is an uncertain science that could be compared to forecasting the weather. But, so too some of the techniques of weather forecasting could also be redeployed to predict the potential desirability of urban agglomerations. It is as though the physical fabric of cities around the globe could be seen as overlaid by an ever-shifting "meteorological" map of desirability—of high-pressure, low pressure, "warm fronts" and "cold fronts"—governed by factors such as social, economic and environmental concerns, by transportational possibilities and lifestyle options. These impulses would then be registered within the physical fabric itself in an endless feedback loop that operates according to a highly complex dynamic. All we can say for certain is that there seems to be a continued desire for the intense corporeality of urban existence, and this, it would appear, has emerged not despite of—but precisely because of—the very disembodied nature of much social interaction today.

Q2: Let me address the question, "Will the individual become increasingly marginalized within a network society?" If we are to follow the logic of recent theories of "swarm intelligence" and "populational thinking", we should recognize that all swarming or flocking behavior is governed not by some top-down authoritarian control, but by bottom-up processes of individual decision making. In other words large-scale networks are based upon the actions of individual operatives. At the same time these individual operatives are themselves influenced by larger-scale concerns. The large scale influences the small scale, and vice versa. We might therefore posit a model of reciprocal presupposition in which the seemingly discrete and opposite tendencies of universalization and differentiation tend to fold into and presuppose one another. In other words, it could be argued that we need not worry about an encroachment to the freedom of the individual within a network society. The more globalized and homogenized systems become, the more they will encourage modes of individual expression.

> Neil Leach is Professor of Architectural Theory at the University of Bath and tutor at the Architectural Association. He has also been Visiting Professor at Columbia University, New York. He is the author of *The Anaesthetics of Architecture* [MIT, 1999], and *Millennium Culture* [Ellipsis, 1999]; editor of *Rethinking Architecture* [Routledge, 1997], *Architecture and Revolution* [Routledge, 1999], *The Hieroglyphics of Space* [Routledge, 2002], *Designing for a Digital World* [Wiley, 2002]; co-editor of *Digital Tectonics* [forthcoming].

BEHIND THE LABEL :

An investigation into the paradoxical assembly line of the global apparel industry

THE GLOBAL ASSEMBLY

by Marisa Yiu

The textile-apparel-retail chain is a dynamic industry, based on an intense and paradoxical mixture of fashion dictated by high-end technology and low-end labor, high-end economy and low-end efficiency. It is a multi-billion dollar business, fusing a low-cost and generic labor force with the high-cost and high-tech fashion industry.

This matrix of connection, in this highly complicated industry provides for simultaneously uncontrollable and delicate spatial conditions. Unlike the once centralized factory of Fordist production, with its mass-production of homogenous goods, our lifestyles and desires of consumption are changed by new technologies and a global sense of organization. This has resonated in a synchronic production that emphasizes the disparities of the *global* and the *local*. *Behind the Label* investigates deep into the unprivileged space of architecture—one that emphasizes global economy and consumer culture within a framework of disparity between the global nature of the apparel industry and the local conditions of apparel manufacture.

Marisa Yiu holds a MArch from Princeton University and a BA from Columbia University. She is currently living and working in New York City.

Behind the Label: the Global Assembly is a continuation of her Graduate Architecture design thesis at Princeton University (advisor Laura Kurgan). BrandSpider *was exhibited at the Whitney Independent Study Program show entitled:* EMPIRE / STATE: artists engaging globalization. *The project research was generated from numerous visits to apparel factories in Dongguan, China.*

Contact: marisa@mksyiu.com

pp. 64-71 "Behind the Label" ©2003 Marisa Yiu, Published by 306090, Inc.

306090 04 03 03 | 03

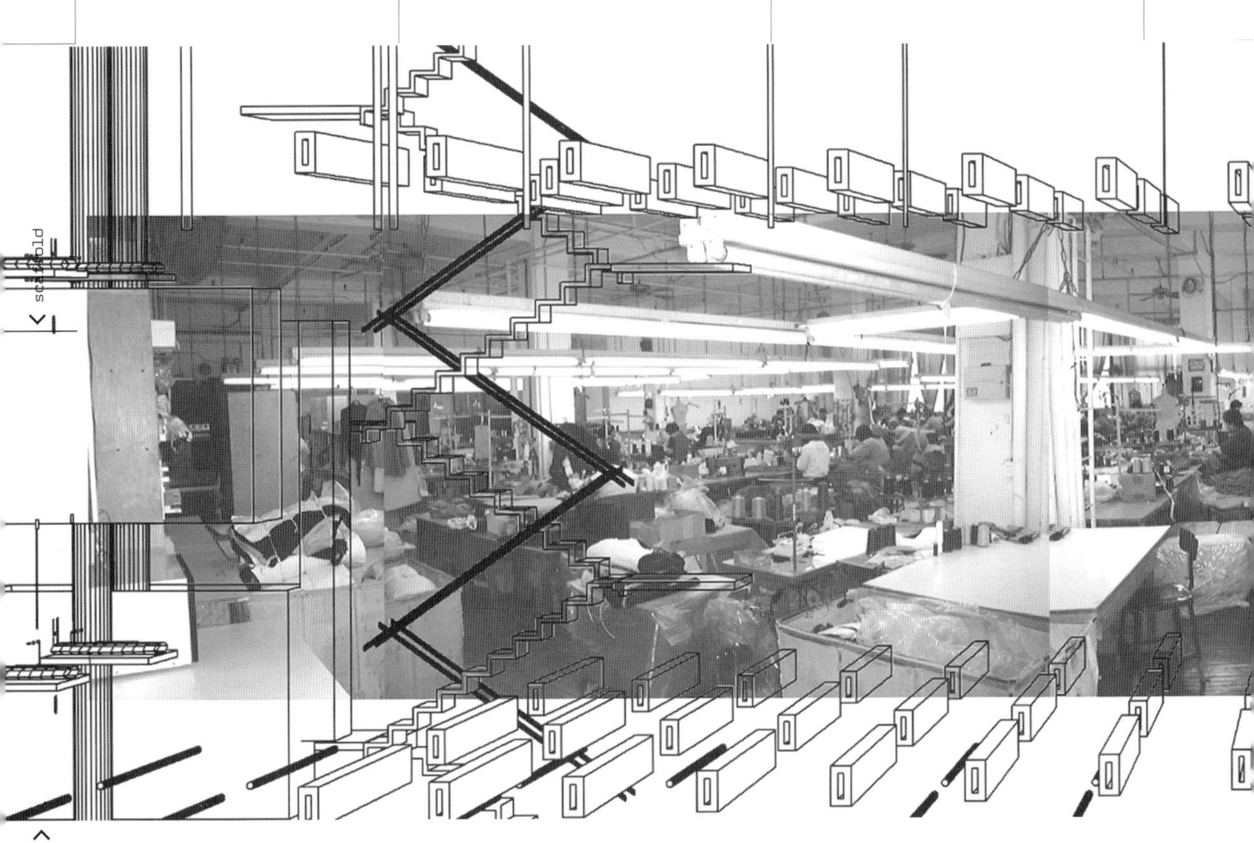

A series of mapping studies and investigative analyses attempted to grapple with this disparity. A web-based survey, asked respondents to randomly select five pieces of garments they owned. Each respondent noted the items manufacturing origin, brand name and type of garment, the retail store it was purchased at, and the city of purchase. A dynamic interface, *BrandSpider* organized and animated the relationships according to categories and cross-referenced information.

The Personal Brain—a software program developed by Brain Technologies—organized the resultant data strings along its network nodes, visually demarcating the item purchased to its far-flung origins of high and low wage regions. When activated, different nodal points shift in and out of the foreground, mobilizing the information along associative chains, suggesting for example the contiguity of familiar high end retailers such as Bloomingdale's with the average hourly wage in a Maquiladoro (apparel factory along the border between U.S + Mexico) or a Chinese export-processing zone.

COUNTRY	APPAREL WAGE [average/hr,$USD]	COUNTRY	APPAREL WAGE [average/hr,$USD]
ASIA		*MIDDLE EAST + AFRICA*	
Bangladesh	0.31	Algeria	1.14
Burma	0.13	Egypt	0.63
China	0.28	Israel	5.65
Hong Kong	4.51	Kenya	0.3
India	0.36	Madagascar	0.29
Indonesia	0.34	Mauritius	1.02
Japan	16.29	Morocco	1.38
Malaysia	1.64	Nigeria	0.51
Pakistan	0.26	Oman	1.51
Philippines	0.62	South Africa	1.26
Singapore	4.11	Tanzania	0.98
Korea Republic	4.18	Zambia	0.38
Sri Lanka	0.41		
Taiwan	5.1	*EUROPE*	
Thailand	1.06	Austria	16.27
Vietnam	0.32	Bulgaria	0.47

306090 04 03 | 03

pp. 64-71 "Behind the Label" ©2003 Marisa Yiu, Published by 306090, Inc.

On a global scale the *BrandSpider* research showed that 49% of the undergarments surveyed were manufactured in Israel, 20% in Indonesia and only 5% in the U.S.A. The most popular brand [GAP] was represented by garments made in factories in twelve different countries: Malaysia, Indonesia, Cambodia, Sri Lanka, The Dominican Republic, The USA, China, Mexico, The Philippines, Zimbabwe, Thailand and Israel. These relationships underpin the interconnectedness of the global garment industry to the very local, specific point of manufacturing.

Seemingly disparate points of manufacturing are connected along the length of the apparel production and consumption line. Although abstract in their networked associations and concealed from the public, these points represent physically real and effective network. On the global scale, they transform themselves into larger spatial problems. Tangibly speaking, the far reaching implication of *the global assembly* crosses multiple country borders as well as multiple factory floors. A physical thread of a garment can pass through a minimum of 38 different hands until it reaches our body. To

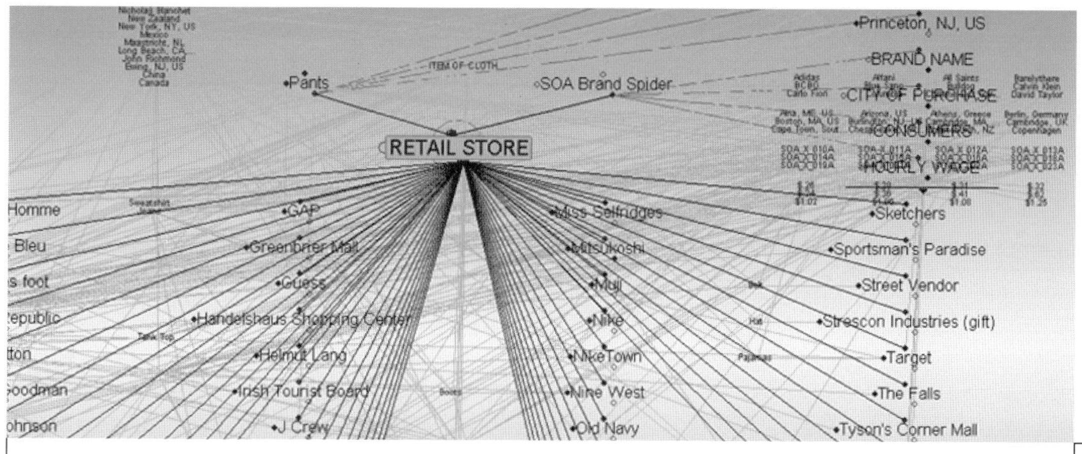

manufacture a pair of jeans takes 30 different tasks on the factory floor.

As Tom Vanderbilt says in *Sneaker Book: a Anatomy of an Industry and an Icon*:

> *An Air Max Penny is designed in Oregon and Tennessee, input is from technicians in South Korea and Taiwan. It is manufactured in South Korea and Indonesia, and made up of 52 components from 5 countries (US - Taiwan - South Korea - Indonesia and Japan) The single shoe touched by 120 pairs of hands.*[1]

Yet he continues to suggest that we have to question the source and root of the label itself:

> *The* Made in U.S.A. *is questionable, as the tag reveals little, since many of its products components may have been manufactured somewhere else, only to be assembled here.*[2]

The *unmasking diagram* [data collected from the NLC (National Labor Committee, NYC)] reveals that on this particular factory floor, there are eight assembly lines for eight different labels of jeans. This factory is located in Mexico, owned by the Chinese, and transported across customs to reach a

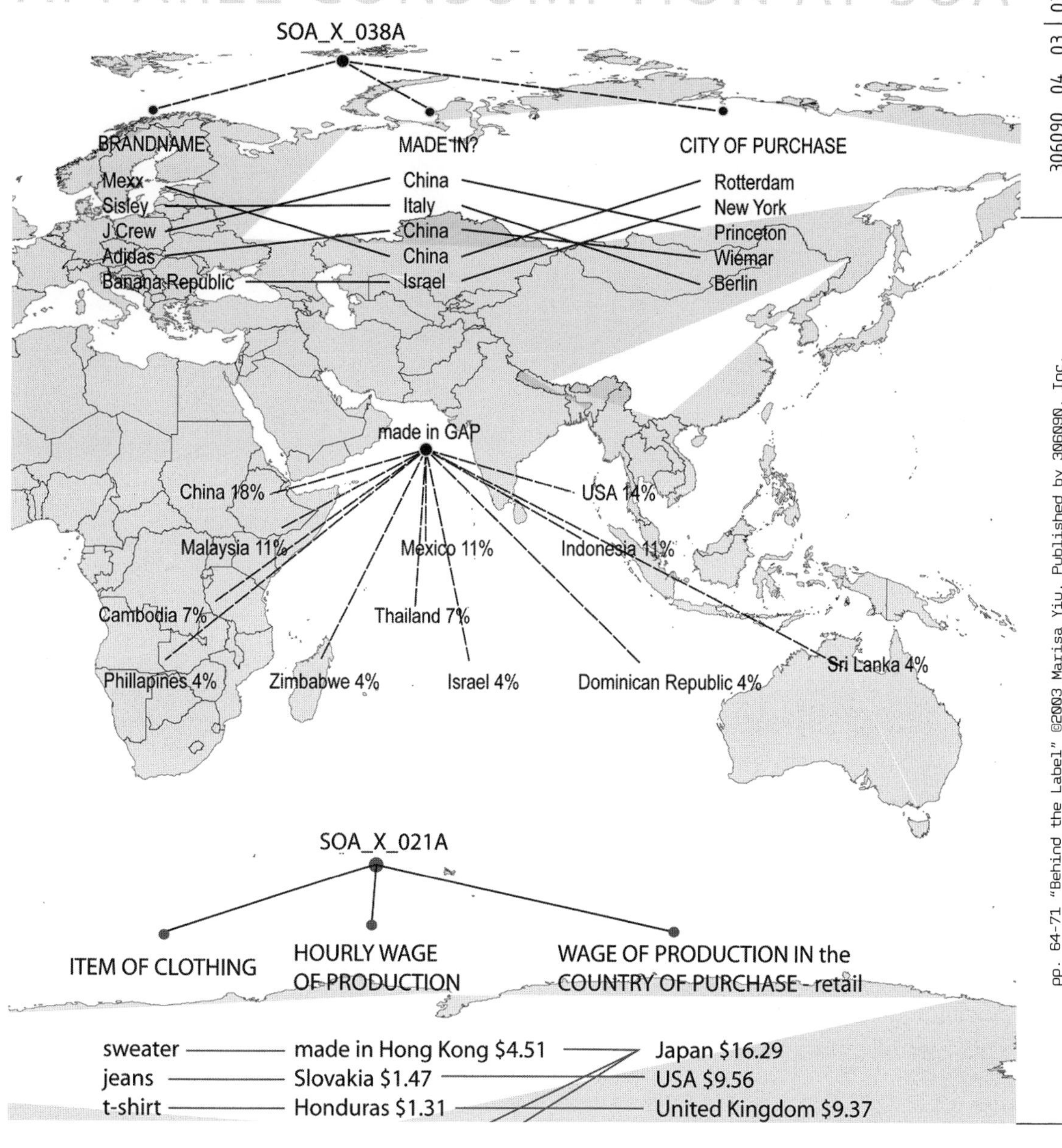

J.C. Penney or other destination by a military based jeans company in the United States. The multiple sites of the production/consumption cycle, link us physically and metaphorically across boundaries, borders and time zones.

As manufacturers and sub-contractors compete against each other for the cheapest, fastest production, the spatial and labor conditions are called into question. Apparel companies are constantly under pressure to re-function their production and to contract out offshore. As these types of operations only require minimal machinery (sewing machines), low-skilled human labor, florescent tube lighting, and efficient assembly units, the generic nature of this space allows it to exist in a multitude of countries. The diagram *behind the label* and *unmasking the factory operation*, maps this comparative data, representing visually the under-normative and sub-standards of clothing manufacturers. As a New York Times article title appropriately stated: "First world appetites collide with third world realities."[3]

306090 04 03 | 03

69

pp. 64-71 "Behind the Label" ©2003 Marisa Yiu, Published by 306090, Inc.

Brandspider: Apparel consumption diagram

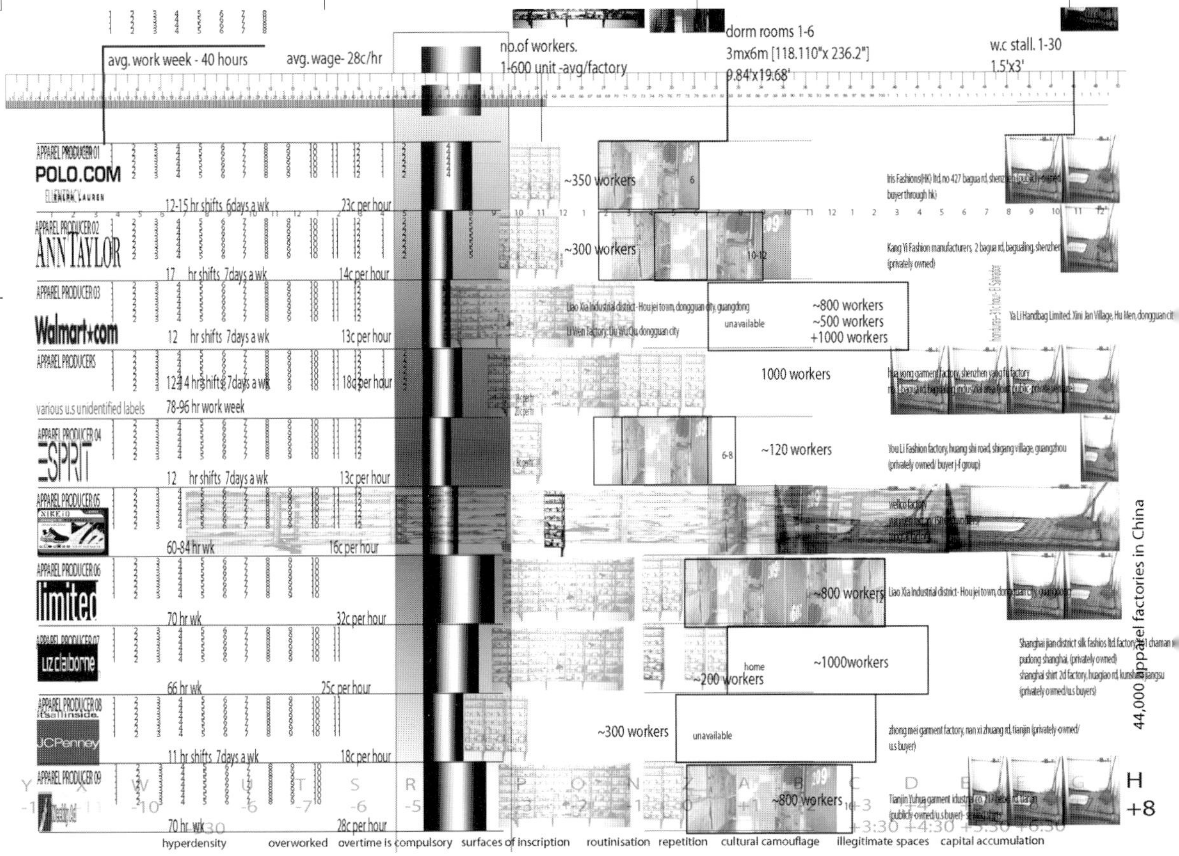

> Made in China diagram

avg. work week - 40 hours

avg. wage- 28c/hr

no. of workers.
1-600 unit -avg/factory

dorm rooms 1-6
3mx6m [118.110"x 236.2"]
9.84'x19.68'

w.c stall. 1-30
1.5'x3'

APPAREL PRODUCER 01
POLO.COM
RALPH LAUREN
12-15 hr shifts 6days a wk — 23c per hour — ~350 workers — 6

APPAREL PRODUCER 02
ANN TAYLOR
17 hr shifts 7days a wk — 14c per hour — ~300 workers — 10-12

APPAREL PRODUCER 03
Walmart*com
12 hr shifts 7days a wk — 13c per hour

APPAREL PRODUCERS
12-14 hrs 7days a wk — 18c per hour
various u.s unidentified labels — 78-96 hr work week

APPAREL PRODUCER 04
ESPRIT
12 hr shifts 7days a wk — 13c per hour

APPAREL PRODUCER 05
60-84 hr wk — 16c per hour

APPAREL PRODUCER 06
limited
70 hr wk — 32c per hour

APPAREL PRODUCER 07
liz claiborne
66 hr wk — 25c per hour

APPAREL PRODUCER 08
itsallinside.
JCPenney
11 hr shifts 7days a wk — 18c per hour

APPAREL PRODUCER 09
70 hr wk — 28c per hour

Iris Fashions(HK) ltd. no 427 bagua rd, shenzhen (publicly-owned,
buyer through hk)

Kang Yi Fashion manufacturers, 2 bagua rd, bagualing, shenzhen
(privately owned)

Liao Xia Industrial district- Hou jei town, dongguan city, guangdong
Li Wen Factory, Liu Wu Qiu, dongguan city
unavailable — ~800 workers / ~500 workers / +1000 workers

Ya Li Handbag Limited, Xini Jan Village, Hu Men, dongguan cit

1000 workers
Hua yong garment factory, shenzhen yang fu factory
no 1 bagua rd, bagualing industrial area (public-private venture)

6-8 — ~120 workers
You Li Fashion factory, huang shi road, shigang village, guangzhou
(privately owned/ buyer j-f group)

velko factory

~800 workers — Liao Xia Industrial district- Hou jei town, dongguan city, guangdong

Shanghai jian district silk fashios ltd. factory, chaman
pudong shanghai (privately owned)
shanghai shirt 2d factory, huaqiao rd, kunshan jiangsu
(privately owned/us buyers)

home
~200 workers — ~1000workers

~300 workers — unavailable
zhong mei garment factory, nan xi zhuang rd, tianjin (privately-owned/
us buyer)

~800 workers
Tianjin Yuhua garment idustry co, 717 hebei rd tianjin
(publicly owned/u.s buyer)

44,000 apparel factories in China

hyperdensity　overworked　overtime is compulsory　surfaces of inscription　routinisation　repetition　cultural camouflage　illegitimate spaces　capital accumulation

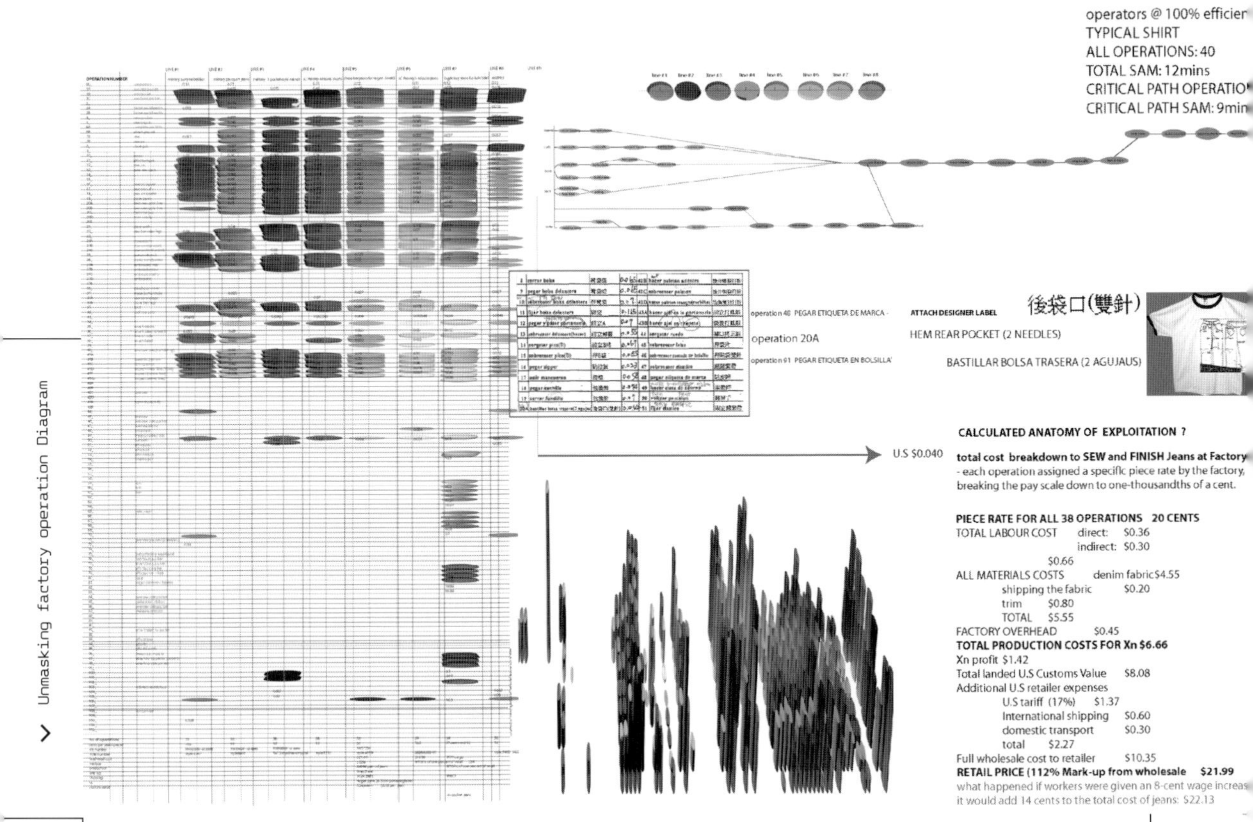

> Unmasking factory operation Diagram

operators @ 100% efficien
TYPICAL SHIRT
ALL OPERATIONS: 40
TOTAL SAM: 12mins
CRITICAL PATH OPERATIO
CRITICAL PATH SAM: 9min

operation 40 PEGAR ETIQUETA DE MARCA -　ATTACH DESIGNER LABEL　後袋口(雙針)

operation 20A　HEM REAR POCKET (2 NEEDLES)

operation 91 PEGAR ETIQUETA EN BOLSILLA'　BASTILLAR BOLSA TRASERA (2 AGUJAUS)

U.S $0.040

CALCULATED ANATOMY OF EXPLOITATION ?

total cost breakdown to SEW and FINISH Jeans at Factory
- each operation assigned a specific piece rate by the factory,
breaking the pay scale down to one-thousandths of a cent.

PIECE RATE FOR ALL 38 OPERATIONS   20 CENTS
TOTAL LABOUR COST　　direct:　$0.36
　　　　　　　　　　　indirect:　$0.30
　　　　　　　　$0.66
ALL MATERIALS COSTS　　denim fabric $4.55
　　　shipping the fabric　　$0.20
　　　trim　　$0.80
　　　TOTAL　　$5.55
FACTORY OVERHEAD　　$0.45
TOTAL PRODUCTION COSTS FOR Xn $6.66
Xn profit $1.42
Total landed U.S Customs Value　　$8.08
Additional U.S retailer expenses
　　　U.S tariff (17%)　　$1.37
　　　International shipping　　$0.60
　　　domestic transport　　$0.30
　　　total　　$2.27
Full wholesale cost to retailer　　$10.35
RETAIL PRICE (112% Mark-up from wholesale　$21.99
what happened if workers were given an 8-cent wage increase
it would add 14 cents to the total cost of jeans: $22.13

306090 04 03 | 03

pp. 64-71 "Behind the Label" ©2003 Marisa Yiu, Published by 306090, Inc.

In the *Made in China* diagram, the relationships of larger *brand companies* (data courtesy of NLC research) show how Polo compared to Wal-mart produces inconsistencies in its *range* of labor conditions: the provision of living space, over-work hours, sub-pay, spatial violations, black production (+ 110 hours of peak production), fly-by night operations, and fire code violations.

Recent research performed by the NLC, highlights the problem of global, yet generic space:

> *Workers are in crowded conditions, ventilation is poor, and they are working 20 hour shifts per day (Sept. 2002, NLC data). This highlights the problem of the global yet generic and extremely local space: the sweatshop. (fire hazards- electrical hazards, health hazards, structural dangers, wage violations, child labor, industrial homework, registration violations, tax irregularities.[4]*

Richard J. Polsonello (New York state director of Labor Standards) states:

> *. . . The logistics of a sweatshop are subject to change and even now sweatshops are locating themselves among the 4000 legitimate sewing shops in the New York City Area Since true sweatshops conform to no measured engineering systems, you find that they are developed based more on economics rather than efficiency. For the most part sweatshops represent the low end of the development spectrum and this may account for their efforts to abuse their employees to maintain an economic survival. It is characteristics of sweatshops do their own wiring and repairs often at the disadvantage of their employees in order to keep costs down. Most sweatshops are undercapitalized businesses. I don't know any studies on the engineering of sweatshops but I do know from experience that sweatshops are much more dangerous to work than legitimate sewing shops in both fiscal and physical matters.[5]*

Due to the elusive nature and the contentious spatial condition of the factory floor, in its fiscal and physical manners the *sweatshop* operates as a system that is rigid yet unpredictable. This system of the undefinitive is problematic and the effects it has on the localized zone generates an uncontrollable, paradoxical and ambiguous space that straddles the line between the legal and the illegal.

These investigative analyses perpetuate the globalization debate. Does economic liberalization promise great wealth or greater misery for the world's poor? Where do architects stand in the shifting balance between politics and business? In these insurmountable questions, the invisible nature of the apparel factory floor, questions the role of architecture in a global manner. What are its boundaries and limits for practitioners of *Architecture*? Can architects claim their role *behind the label*? As Naomi Klein says, perhaps not:

> *The gated factories remain tucked away in remote places, less able to pose a direct challenge to the seductive rhetoric of the borderless world.[6]*

We live in a world of dynamic transition that affects almost every detail of what we do. For better or worse, we are being propelled into a global order no one fully comprehends, with effects that are impacted upon us. It is wrong to think of globalization as solely concerning the big systems and the world financial order.

Globalization is not only about what is *out there*, remote and far away from the individual, but also about what is *in here*, a phenomenon influencing all intimate aspects of everyday life.

End Notes:

[1] Tom Vanderbilt, "Sneaker Book: Anatomy of an Industry and an Icon", The New Work Press, NY, 1998.

[2] Tom Vanderbilt, "Sneaker Book: Anatomy of an Industry and an Icon", The New Work Press, NY, 1998.

[3] Leslie Kaufman and David Gonzalez, "First World Appetites Collide with Third World Realities", New York Times, April 2001.

[4] National Labor Committee, "Working for Disney in Bangladesh: a Dungeon, not a Magic Kingdom", September 2002, <http://www.nlcnet.org/bangladesh/reports/dungeon.pdf>

[5] Personal email discourse between author and Richard J. Polsonello

[6] Naomi Klein, "Fences and Windows: Dispatches from the Frontlines of the Globalization Debate", Picador, NY, 2002, p 23.

SARAJEVO UNDER

NO MORE SQUARES, NO MORE STREETS
no more sidewalks, no more windows -
life moved into the cellars, the garages
and the courtyards of the surrounding
urban fabric.

A new energy emerges in a war-torn, yet optimistic city

SIEGE

by Sebastiano Olivotto

Sarajevo in the 20th Century

There is a passage in Joseph Conrad's Heart of Darkness that describes the Congo as a white indefinite area on the map. When I went to Sarajevo in 1999 it was like landing in a white speck of color; having emerged from under the war news reflectors it had became a mysterious unknown place.

Reconstruction, it seemed, was going to start with the goal of rebuilding, and restoring an international interest in this new capital.

Sarajevo is a city that more than any other has experienced the trauma of contradiction from its many sides. A melting pot, and home of Orthodox, Muslim, and Catholic worship sites, it is the place where the east and the west meet. While the map of Europe shifted and twisted, Sarajevo moved from a border city to a central capital of history, the place where the 20th century started and ended. Sarajevo ended the last century with four years under a cruel and punishing siege. This condition generated a disjunction and fragmentation of the fabric of the city, through the perpetual violation of all communication and distribution systems. At the same time it generated a systematic and methodical destruction of the most vital buildings of the city.

Sebastiano Olivotto graduated Cum Laude in Architectural Planning and Design at the I.U.A.V. in Venice. Olivotto was Bevilacqua La Masa Foundation Artist Fellowship Prize Winner in 1998; his works have been exhibited in several national and international group shows. Olivotto is presently working on an editorial project on the New York architectural design firm S.I.T.E. for the Italian publishing house "Universale di Architettura," founded and directed by Bruno Zevi.

N.U.L. BiH Sarajevo was completed under the supervision of Franco Purini, Lebbeus Woods and Paolo Colusso. 3D Model by Sebastiano Olivotto and Giovanni Scalcino. Rendering by Sebastiano Testoni. Photography by Sebastiano Olivotto. Special Thanks to Ivan Straus, Sead Golos, Dom Engineering, National And University Library of Bosnia-Herzegovina, Enes Kujundzic, Zlatko Disdarevic, and Giorgia Salmaso.

Contact: olivotto@artificialprojects.com

306090 04 03 | 03

pp. 72-77 "Sarajevo Under Siege" ©2003 Sebastiano Olivotto, Published by 306090, Inc.

Axonometric of the N.U.L.

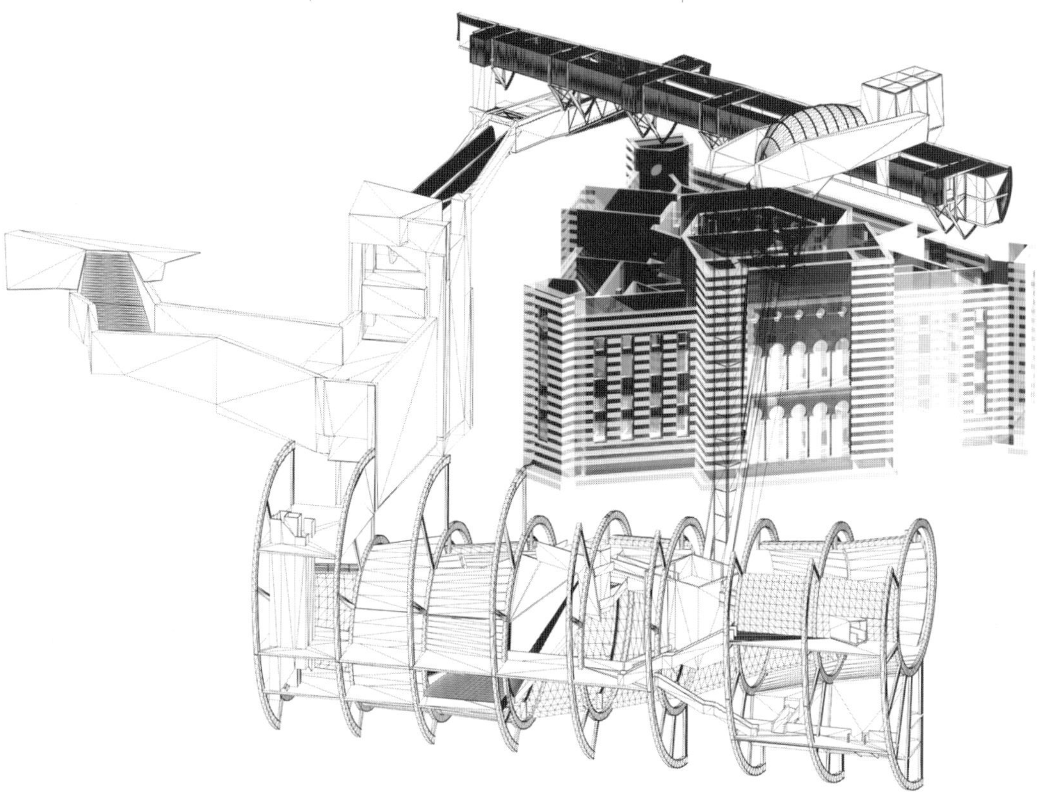

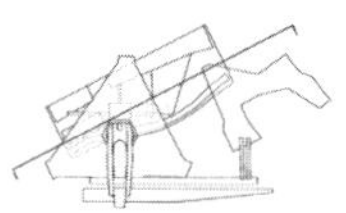

Longitudinal Section

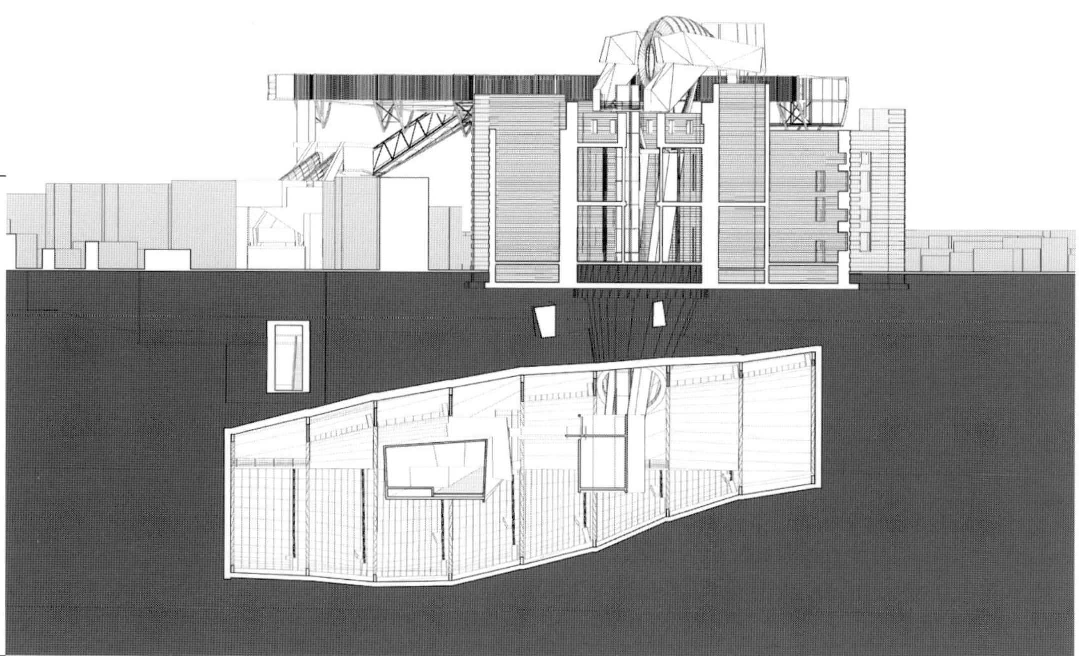

306090 04 03 | 03

Mass Urbicide

This *urbicide* was dramatically efficient in its destabilization of Sarajevo as traditional roles of city elements were turned upside down. The siege plunged this place into an irrational and chaotic alternate reality where what was working before had no more importance, where survival created and actuated new collective behaviors and extreme environments. The effect of these necessary and new behaviors was the reinterpretation of architectural and urban typologies, now investing unusual spaces with usual functions.

No more squares, streets or sidewalks, no more windows—life moved into the cellars, the garages and the courtyards of the surrounding urban fabric.

When war and all these realities left Sarajevo at the end of the conflict, it left as its legacy a powerful latent ground condition for the research of a new aesthetic.

A Library through the Ruins of History

This project proposes a new National and University Library for the young state of Bosnia-Herzegovina (N.U.L. BiH), a country with a tremendous cultural heritage. Indeed, the literary culture and physical history of books is particular to the country's heritage. The great treasures of this culture were lost in the burning of the Vijecnica building during war time. The N.U.L. BiH rises from the ancient and damaged Vijecnica Building—it is a place for the reconstruction and protection of that heritage.

As a new National Library in Sarajevo, this project juxtaposes two fundamental issues. The first involves the re-interpretation of the library as a typology in the light of recent technological advances in the storage, collection and display of data. The second is the relationship the N.U.L. BiH should have with the city in light of its recent dramatic history. The thematic intersection of these two issues has brought about the development of two different architectural realities within a single, coherent project.

The N.U.L. BiH reflects the need for an archive that an invaluable heritage demands, but at the same time is conscious of today's technological and communication reality and of its continual evolution. These two realities, in turn, reflect two contemporary means through which one accesses information and thereby formulates knowledge: the analog (books) and the digital (computers). Rather than fuse these two means (and risk diluting their separate potencies) the N.U.L. BiH develops two main spheres which summarize separately these two means.

The N.U.L. BiH proposes a traditional library and a *mediatheque*, a digital information storage and access hub. The two programs are respectively placed beneath and above the wreck of the original library. The city—and more particularly the damaged architecture—represent the edge space and at the same time the linking space between the two parts. The central court of the old library is the site of a new tower that links the underground program vertically with the aerial one. Providing a vision of the ruins, it is a passage that brings with it the very essence of the experience of history. The space of the drama of war becomes the space of change and of metamorphosis—the nexus between past and future.

The effort was in creating two architectural languages, each able to express the two realities— the contemporary or digital, and the traditional or analog—and to relate them with the post-war reality of the site in Sarajevo. A vertical development was suggested by the fact that the original library, after its destruction, had become an empty space without horizontal elements. Such destruction has highlighted the role of the library to safeguard information and knowledge. The library must not only be an organizational space but also a protective one, a shelter for cultural and physical heritage.

The Archive

As books are eventually replaced by digital forms of communication, the physical text will acquire more and more of a sacred value. The underground portion of the library, which is related to the concept of an archive, is a strong and enclosed form that cannot be modified or expanded; accordingly it adopts a *complete* character as a collection. It is an organic space into which the archive is placed and accessed by a mechanical system—here machine and hardware are still the protagonists. In contrast, the aerial portion of the protagonist is software: the *mediatheque* finds its place in the air, where the interception of digital, electronic fluxes and changing platforms of information acquisition is reflected by

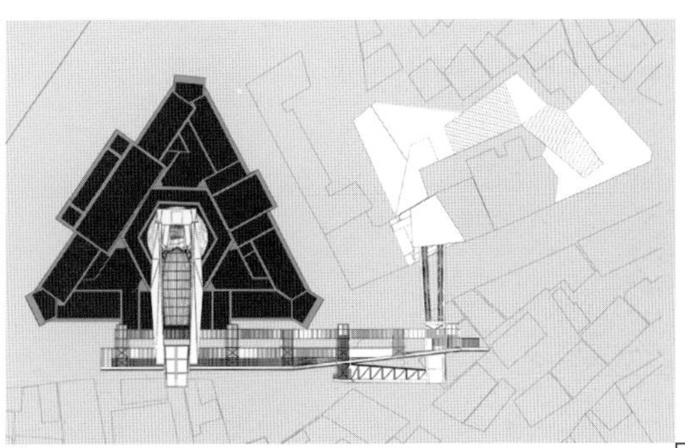

pp. 72-77 "Sarajevo Under Siege" ©2003 Sebastiano Olivotto, Published by 306090, Inc.

∧ Context View of the N.U.L. in Sarajevo

> Perspectival of the N.U.L.

> Aerial View of the N.U.L.

a lightweight architecture. This aerial portion is an expandable fragment of a larger, growing system that, like a network will gradually spread into and over the city.

The *mediatheque*, as elaborated in its architectural organization, is a derivation of the underground portion but differs from it as an architecture that duplicates and dismantles in form in order to connect itself to the urban fabric. This is how the aerial program manages to break a purely linear path, suggesting rather a system of paths that create a cycle, placing visitors to the N.U.L. BiH within a perpetual journey.

The cyclic nature of these paths lends the system a non-linear organization, and at the same time it gives the N.U.L. BiH a non-hierarchical characteristic. The organization develops into a conceptual and functional differentiation of the spaces that does not set a hierarchy of values and architectonical images, but remains in different parts and elements, clearly recognizable in their iconography. The images are independent, but at the same time they are associated within a complexity that they themselves contribute to create.

The project underscores a set of tectonic elements and images. Something like the characters of a drama, they all strive for the promise of protagonism, developing the plot through a continuous play of coalitions and abandonment.

The Event

The power of the plot and its communicative elements represent the fundamental conditions for a project that proposes an architecture of the event. N.U.L. BiH is not meant as a celebrative or memorial architecture, on the contrary it is like an object that appears when the event is already over, like an actor that appears on the stage stealing the scene from his worn-out colleague, avoiding in so doing a temporal emptiness and assuring continuity in the timeline of the story.

The play of roles in this discussion of the N.U.L. BiH are not at all haphazard, in fact the project resembles a big technological puppet—a digitally mediated marionette that brings with it the whole drama of its rich and complex past, present, and optimistic future.

306090 04 03 | 03

pp. 72–77 "Sarajevo Under Siege" ©2003 Sebastiano Olivotto, Published by 306090, Inc.

Detail of N.U.L. Circulation >

ARCHITECTURE FOR

Cameron Sinclair discusses the Mobile HIV/AIDS Clinic Competition, AFH and the state of humanitarian architecture

306090 Interviews the Founding Director of Architecture for Humanity

HUMANITY

> 1. The concept of *outreach* seems to be a guiding force for Architecture for Humanity. Can you describe what implications this has had, and what other factors have motivated your organization to engage some of the most complex and controversial issues of our time?

The term *outreach* does describe the goals of our current project to tackle the spread of HIV/AIDS in sub-Saharan Africa. Each project however, presents its own set of variables and requires a different approach. What our projects share in common is primarily an effort to create opportunities for architects and designers from around the world to connect with community groups and relief organizations and hopefully build sustainable, well-designed structures they would not otherwise have the resources to implement.

In general we have selected projects on the basis of need and feasibility—each project must also have a design component. You describe the issues we have focused on as *controversial*, in many ways they are not. In fact, because there is a broad-based consensus on what needs to be done by experts in the field, these issues represent an ideal opportunity for architects and designers to utilize their skills and expertise.

Cameron Sinclair is the Founding Director of Architecture For Humanity. He was trained as an architect at the University of Westminster and at the Bartlett School of Architecture in London. During his studies, he developed an interest in social, cultural and humanitarian design. His postgraduate thesis focused on providing shelter to New York's homeless population through sustainable, transitional housing. After completing his studies, he moved to New York where he has worked as a designer and project architect.

Since 1996, Sinclair has worked on projects in more than 20 countries in Eastern Europe, and Africa as well as the United Kingdom, Russia, and the United States. As a project architect with Gensler in New York, Sinclair helped design the award-winning School of the International Center of Photography in Manhattan and was a key member in the disaster recovery team for Lehman Brothers after terrorist attacks destroyed their offices on September 11th.

Sinclair has also been a guest critic and lecturer at a number of schools and colleges, including Pratt Institute, Cranbrook College of Art and the University of Pennsylvania Graduate School of Architecture. Last year he was the keynote speaker at the ACSA/AIA Teachers' Seminar and spoke at the Dean's Forum at West Point. In 2003, he is scheduled to speak at the Structures for Inclusion III conference and at the 53rd annual Aspen International Design Conference. Sinclair is the 2002 recipient of the Nice Modernist Award by Dwell Magazine and the 2002 Innovator Award by eKornes. He is also featured in the forthcoming book, Soul Purpose: 40 People Who Are Changing the World for the Better.

Web: www.architectureforhumanity.org

Contact: csinclair@architectureforhumanity.org

pp. 78-85 "Mobile HIV/AIDS Clinic for Africa" ©2003 306090, Published by 306090, Inc.

Africa Under Siege: Craig Coulton and Marcel Botha [London, UK + Cape Town, South Africa]

306090 04 03 | 03

pp. 78-85 "Mobile HIV/AIDS Clinic for Africa" ©2003 306090, Published by 306090, Inc.

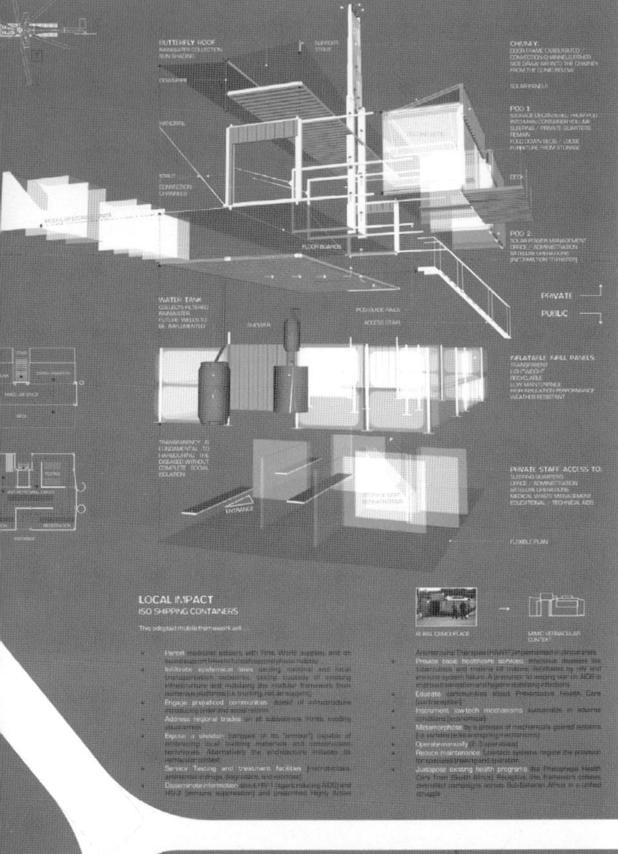

PHASED INTEGRATION

. . . there is Hope for Africa · Thembela Africa

The recent Mobile HIV/AIDS Health Clinic for Africa initiative is a perfect example where it became apparent during time we spent in Africa, that one of the major factors inhibiting medical professionals from treating HIV/AIDS is the inability to access vast areas of the continent with adequately equipped facilities. On the surface this is a very apparent architectural problem yet the criteria could not have been developed without the knowledge and expertise from medical teams actually on the ground as well as researchers based here and in Africa. Over the course of a year we further consulted with a large number of doctors in the field and other relief groups including: John Hopkins University School of Hygiene and Public Health, voluntary counseling and testing facilities in Zimbabwe, Kenya, Ghana and South Africa, the World Health Organization, UNESCO, UNAIDS, Southern Africa AIDS Information Dissemination Service, and the Population Council.

In addition to instigating design initiatives and competitions, Architecture for Humanity also aims to promote humanitarian and social design through advocacy and education programs. To that end, we have developed a network of professional architects, designers, urban planners, students and faculty willing to invest time, energy and expertise to promote humanitarian and social architecture. In some cases we act as a liaison, connecting relief organizations and community groups with interested professionals in specific regions to address urgent humanitarian needs. For example, on a number of projects—including *mine-clearance* programs in the Balkans, earthquake recovery assistance in Turkey and refugee housing on the borders of Afghanistan—we have referred relief organizations to local architects and design professionals.

Architecture for Humanity also works closely with faculty and students to develop curriculum and share design principles. At the university level, architecture and design programs around the world have used our competitions and design criteria as a model for semester-long projects in social and humanitarian architecture.

Younger students have also benefited from our design initiatives. In conjunction with both the Transitional Housing competition and the Mobile AIDS/HIV health clinic competition, Architecture for Humanity has sponsored workshops for high school and elementary school students. These workshops explained the need for intervention and supplied students with materials to design their own solutions.

Mobile intervention

Design For A Mobile HIV/AIDS Clinic For Africa

2002   Architecture for Humanity

The Idea

Mobility: … Quality of being mobile....Movement of people , as from one social group, class or level to another....quality of moving freely"

The American Heritage® Dictionary of the English Language, Fourth Edition

Not only the creation of a clinic to provide neccessary healthcare , not only coming and going - as Aids is not coming with the clinic and is not going with the clinic - but rather bringing the frame for the integration of community, the creation of a platform for initial activities to be grown, a possibility of transition and multiplication, at the same time the creation of a landmark to set the change!

The Task

A clinic mobile within rural areas, being operable as mini clinic using one box operated by 2-4 professionals, as maxi clinic, using two boxes with the option of a focus on medical supply or information and dissemination, operated by 4-8 professionels, or as extension for an existing stationary clinic.

The Elements

The Wall:
Being created by the community itself using local materials, having the same shape at every location, providing a common platform, which can be used for different purposes without the clinic (exhibitions, meeting point, teaching), forming the clinic as being the element providing additional semi-outdoor spaces while operating the clinic, building a landmark to set a new sign... Start off!

The Gate:
Marking the transition within the wall, as changing from one side to another, not only spacially but intellectually....Change!

The Box:
Containing the clinic as a whole including all functions (transport - housing - medical support - teaching and dissemination), each main function represented by an extendable unit, using the wall as enclosure for extending semi-outdoor spaces.

The Units:
Each one representing a single function, the Medical Unit, containing storage for medical supply and equipment, foldable couches for treatment, laboratory and cooling facilities for medication, the Information Unit, containing storage facilities for distribution material, condoms, posters etc, a working place, providing space for guidance, teaching, and distribution, the Personal Unit, containing foldable beds for a maximum of 4 Professionals, a small kitchen unit, dining table, storage and a sanitary unit.

The operation concept

Operated by medical Professionals but integrated participation by the community, e.g. schools for collecting recycling material filling the wall (wood, brick, bamboo, cans...), local labor building the wall, setting up the clinic when arriving, being used not only as medical health care station but for secondary services such as guidance, welfare, psychological treatment, employment, contacts to orphan homes.

Examples for wall fillings:

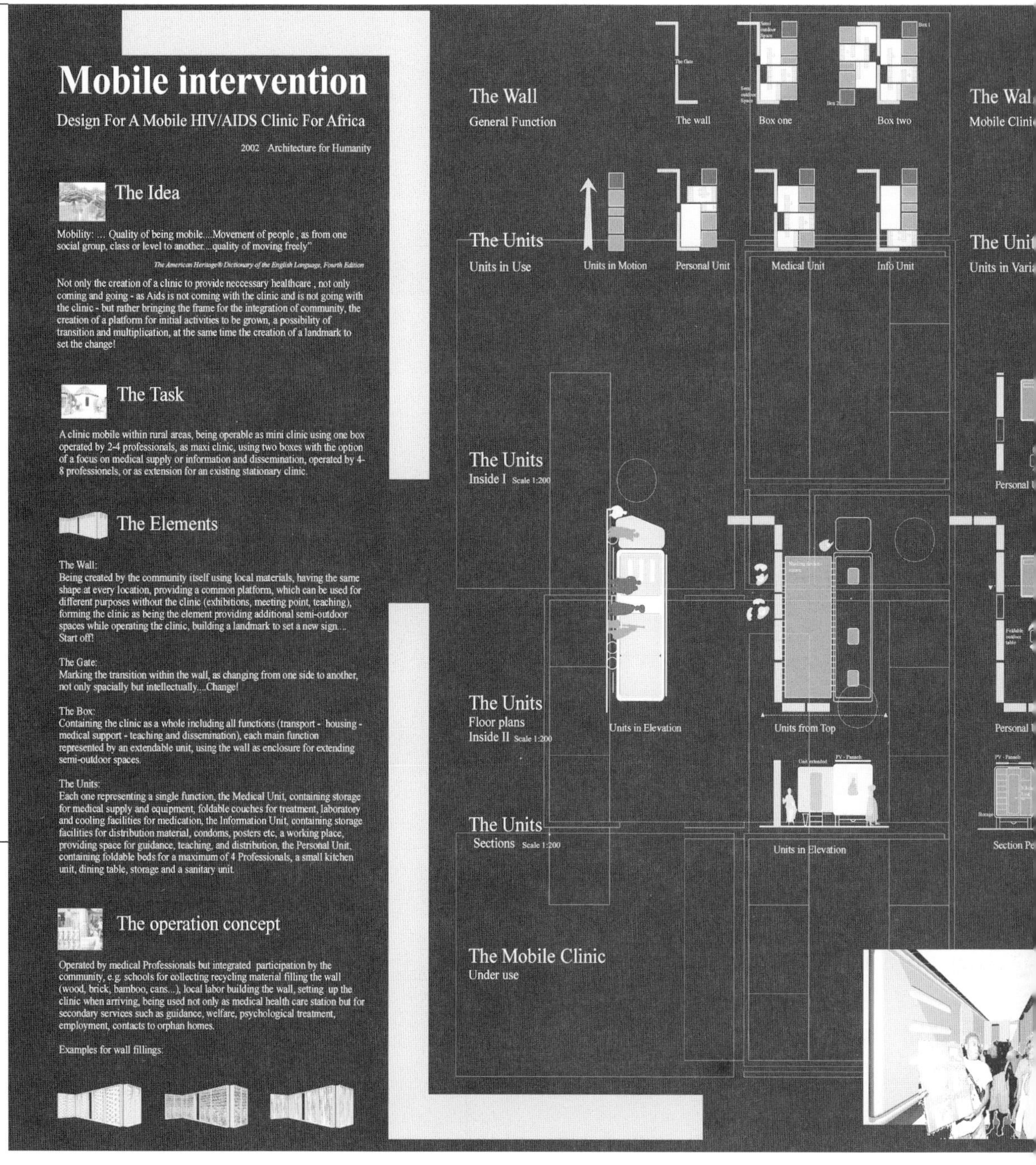

306090 04 03 | 03

pp. 78-85 "Mobile HIV/AIDS Clinic for Africa" ©2003 306090, Published by 306090, Inc.

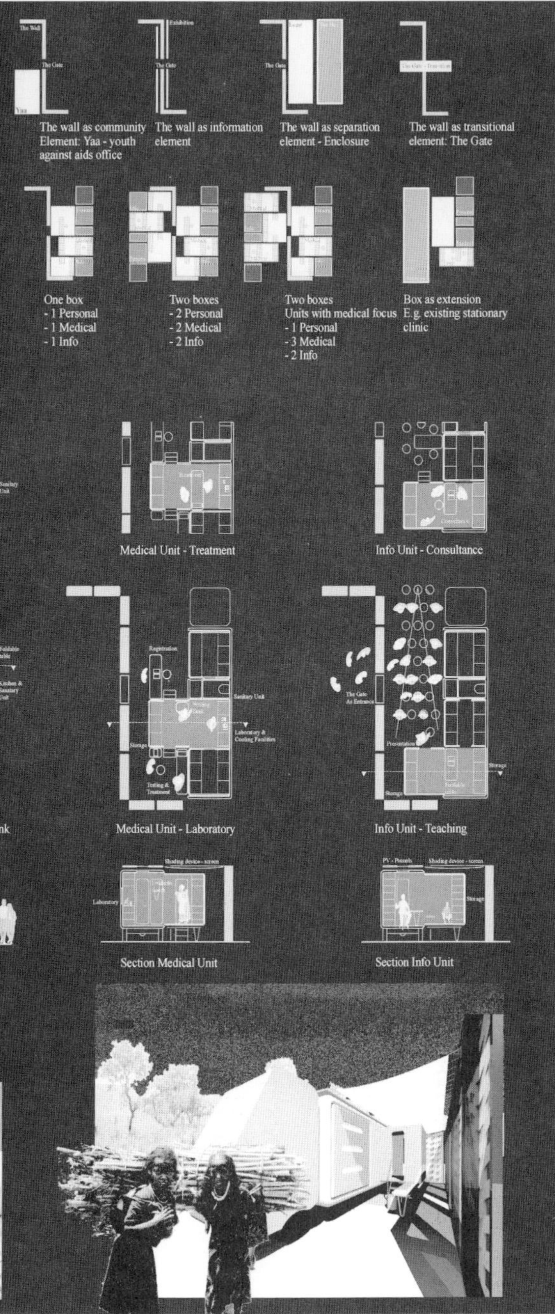

Finally, Architecture for Humanity has participated in a range of workshops, seminars, conferences, and other learning opportunities for the architectural and design community. As we grow, we will continue to foster collaboration between students, faculty, practicing professionals, relief organizations and community groups. Hopefully this work will not only create a global network of socially aware designers but help to foster public appreciation for the many ways that architecture and design can improve lives.

> 2. During the last 15 years, globalization and has brought immense wealth and development to the far reaches of the earth. Never before have we had the ability to understand the global condition with such detail—whether it is environmental change, migration, disease or sprawl. What effect has this knowledge had on our notion of *responsibility*—both as a local and global necessity?

It is as much an opportunity as a responsibility.

> 3. The UN Population Division projects that 60% of the world's population will live in urban agglomerations by the year 2030. What implications might this have for future patterns of growth, settlement and survival? What are the possibilities? What is the future of cities?

Defining cities and the nature of the cityscape is slightly outside of our realm of our work. However the continued natural growth and increased movement of populations into the urban environment has huge ramifications on the nature of what and how we build. Essential structures of everyday life will have to adapt to the increased changes in populations and the nature of how we lead our lives. We will eventually become a society driven by service industries and highly dispersed networks.

> 4. The design professions seem to have marginalized themselves in recent years—the turn of the millennium was marked by a decadent blend of massive corporate development, unmitigated growth and degradation of our natural resources. How might this situation be translated into a positive force for change?

I'm not sure if the design profession has become marginalized as much as further misunderstood. With the unprecedented growth during the nineties came the idea of architecture as fashionable commodity. Within the public realm, design is seen as either reserved only for the privileged or as a status symbol for corporations. Perhaps worse than our desire to embrace this trend is how we have been willing to undercut each other, to the point of accepting little or no fee in order to clamor for the few choice projects that might propel careers onto the covers of magazines and the inclusion into the hip world of pop culture. Recent mainstream coverage has even included covering the stylish eye wear of certain architects and restaurant reviews by designers *in the know.*

Where resources and expertise are scarce—innovative, sustainable and collaborative design can make a difference.

—Cameron Sinclair

First Place Design Concept

Mikkel Beedholm, Mads Hansen and Jan Søndergaard
KHRAS Architects, Virium, Denmark.

This design by architects of the Danish firm KHRAS met the criteria of the competition on a number of levels. The frame is designed to fit within the footprint of a standard container and can therefore be moved easily using various modes of transportation. A satellite dish and water collection system make the unit self-sustaining, and a locking system enables health workers in the field to secure equipment and supplies at night and during transport. At the same time, while the light-weight, metal skeleton is universal in feeling, materials woven into the frame add local texture. "The sequencing was well thought out, and we really responded to the size and scale of this approach" said jury member Toshiko Mori, professor in practice and chair of the Harvard Design School. "In Africa, especially in remote areas, you don't just get a spare part from down the road. So instead of one solution we wanted to come up with a system," explained Mads Hansen, a member of the design team. "If you want to implement this all you need is a simple frame." [text credit: www.architectureforhumanity.com]

Along with the globalization has come the automation of the design world. The last decade has led to a highly computer literate generation of designers thrust into the workforce only to find themselves as nothing more than CAD Monkeys—cutting and pasting design elements from one project to the next. The studio-style creative process has all but left the profession, and the hierarchical ladder has become even harder to ascend. It is no wonder that many young professionals have decided to leave the profession in search of a more creative design process.

There has also been an awkward split between the ideals of design as pure art and those determined by finance. However, somewhere amongst the doyens of the design world and the corporate juggernauts is an ever-growing band of critical practices that for the last few decades have been often overlooked. From the visionary drive of Samuel 'Sambo' Mockbee and the Rural Studio or Bunker Roy and the 'Barefoot architects of Tilonia' to the work of community based designers such as the Detroit Collaborative Design Center. These designers have seen the potential to become more involved and to create change where it is needed most.

> 5. What is the role of the *architect-as-leader* in this process?

Although in many projects at times it seems that we are the lowest on the totem pole, the reality is that with any good building the lead on a project is more often than not taken by the architect. We have the unique ability to translate ideas to a myriad of people, collaborate within large and diverse groups, develop and build teams with a variety of expertise and most importantly to properly implement a project within a strategic time frame.

Within many critical practices the role of the architect or designers also has had to adapt depending on the task at hand. In some projects the community is at loggerheads with city officials and cannot communicate its needs. The designer may take the role a liaison, translating the project in a way both parties can understand.

6. Refugees continue to flee famine, poverty, disease and war; ethnic battles rage on; the global divide between rich and poor continues to widen; and the HIV/AIDS epidemic is devastating entire populations, with no end in sight. Why is it important for design professionals to engage these problems? What possible role can architects, engineers, artists, etc. play in a world that appears to be out of control?

The skills and knowledge we gain from working in the design profession can and should have a direct affect on some of the most important and serious global issues facing our time. Environmentally, we have the responsibility to make informed choices in the materials we use, the way we build and where we build. These choices affect issues beyond that of deforestation or using products that emit huge amounts of toxic pollutants into the air, such as the forced migration of local people due to massive development.

Their design skills, ability to communicate ideas and experience working with people from all walks of life, afford architects and designers a unique opportunity to help others. Health care, education, the arts, business and government necessarily require structures in which services can be provided and ideas exchanged. We believe that where resources and expertise are scarce—innovative, sustainable and collaborative design can make a difference.

Furthermore the profession has the opportunity to take a lead in shaping not only the physical landscape but also the potential for political change. There are instances where innovative design that could help the lives of many has been thwarted or caught up in the red tape of pre-existing policy. Instead of waiting for those currently in charge to take the initiative, architects and designers, who at times are the most informed to do so, should try to influence, shape and potentially rewrite the policy not only for the good of a particular project but for the industry as a whole.

> 7. Give us Cameron Sinclair's definition of *humanitarian architecture*.

I'm not sure there is a true definition for either the word *humanitarian* or *architecture* both are very subjective in their nature and equally dangerous to qualify. If you strip away the ego, the *archi-lingo* and the philosophies of design, the role of architecture is to provide shelter.

Our profession embodies far more than simply creating inspiring spaces. It is about innovating and striving to achieve a better environment, in which we live, work and play. Whether that is done by taking on the role of developer, community liaison, politician or simply that of the designer we have the unique opportunity of directly affecting the lives of those around us and taking on the responsibility that comes with it.

306090 04 03 | 03

pp. 78-85 "Mobile HIV/AIDS Clinic for Africa" ©2003 306090, Published by 306090, Inc.

TROJAN GOAT

The UVA Solar Decathlon Team

306090 04 03 | 03

pp. 86-91 "Trojan Goat" ©2003 John Quale, Published by 306090, Inc.

Pushing the boundaries of design and engineering—students collaborate on the design and construction of a highly innovative solar-powered jewel box

by John Quale

The sun is the source of all forms of energy on the earth—from fossil fuels such as natural gas and petroleum, which become depleted over time, to renewable forms of energy such as biomass, wind, and solar power. Each day the sun directly radiates more than 10,000 times the amount of energy required in the world. Efficient and environmentally-benign methods of harvesting this direct solar radiation are clearly the wave of the future.

The United States—the world's largest economy—generates and uses more energy than any other nation. Not surprisingly, the U.S. is also the world's single largest generator of greenhouse gas emissions. Over one-third of these emissions are produced by buildings alone. The average single-family home in the U.S. emits more than 22,000 pounds of carbon dioxide each year (from the electricity generated by utilities to run the home, and oil or gas powered appliances and equipment in the home). This is more than twice the amount emitted by the typical American car. The reality is that inefficient McMansions are more harmful to the environment than gas guzzling SUV's.

Over one hundred architecture and engineering students, faculty members, and volunteers were involved in the design, planning, fund raising and construction of this project. Although it is impossible to mention them all here—it is important to note that without their dedicated involvement, this project would never have been possible.

Trojan Goat Student Project Management Team:
Adam Ruffin: MArch '02, SARC. Dave Click: MS '03, SEAS. Charlotte Barrows: BSArch '02, SARC. Josh Dannenberg: BSArch '02, SARC. Ben Dorrier: BS '02, SEAS. Tim Sweeney: BS '03, SEAS.

Faculty Advisors:
John Quale: Assistant Professor, SARC, architecture advisor
Paxton Marshall: Associate Professor, SEAS, engineering advisor
Dan Pearce: Research Scientist, SEAS, engineering advisor

Special Thanks:
UVA School of Architecture and School of Engineering and Applied Sciences—Karen Van Lengen: Dean and Edward E. Elson Professor, SARC. Richard Miksad: Dean and Thomas M. Linville Professor, SEAS. Judith Kinnard: Associate Professor and Chair, Architecture, SARC. Bill Sherman: Associate Professor and Associate Dean for Academics, SARC. Jason Johnson: Assistant Professor, SARC.

Major Sponsors: Martin-Horn General Contractors, UVA Alumni Assoc. Class of 1995, Elwood R. Quesada Educational Foundation, The University of Virginia.

John Quale is currently an Assistant Professor of Architecture at the University of Virginia where he teaches design and photography. He was the Architecture Advisor to the UVA Solar Decathlon Team. Quale holds a B.A. in Asian Studies. He received his Master of Architecture from UVa in 1993. Quale and his wife Sara Osborne, a landscape architect, have established Q&O Design.

Five possible ways to address this problem:

1. Build more efficient buildings by maximizing insulation and minimizing air infiltration.

2. Minimize energy loads by designing more efficient lighting, appliances and equipment (and offer incentives to encourage Americans to install these items).

3. Make it more attractive for Americans to harvest the sun directly—using equipment that converts solar radiation into electricity (photovoltaics) or allows the sun to collect heat for hot water and space heating.

4. Use the principles of climate responsive design and create buildings that can heat up and cool down without mechanical equipment.

5. Use intelligent design to encourage a greater awareness of the way the sun participates in our daily lives.

The responsibility rests on the shoulders of many—architects, politicians, utility executives, homeowners, building code officials, builders. As design professionals, including architects and engineers, a special aspect of this responsibility lies with us. We must lead the construction industry towards more responsible, intelligent and efficient buildings.

Solar Decathlon

In an effort to address these issues, the U.S. Department of Energy recently organized the first-ever Solar Decathlon. A national competition to design and build an 800 square foot house powered entirely by the sun, the 2002 Solar Decathlon brought together fourteen universities from across the U.S. to compete in ten events focused on energy efficient house design. The teams assembled their houses on the National Mall in Washington DC during the fall of 2002.

A team of architecture and engineering students at the University of Virginia participated in the event. Over the course of two years, more than 100 students spent countless hours designing, debating and building. They collaborated on all aspects of the process—from schematic design to construction; from fund raising to equipment specification. The *School of Architecture* and the *School of Engineering and Applied Science* integrated the project into their curricula, so that students could work together in and out of the classroom to put theories of sustainability into practice.

Along the way, they were forced to question their ideas about *sustainable* design. The team negotiated a complicated maze of ethical, aesthetic, technical and financial issues. The toughest situation an ecologically-minded designer faces is

306090 04 03|03

pp. 86-91 "Trojan Goat" ©2003 John Quale, Published by 306090, Inc.

Visitors waiting to tour The Trojan Goat ∧
on the Mall in Washington DC

students worked together to put theories of sustainability into practice

when circumstances challenge a design idea or a philosophical position. The challenge is compounded when the *designer* is not an individual, but a large group loosely organized as a democracy. Decisions that require judgment and a careful consideration of trade-offs become more complex when they have to be made by a diverse team of people—each with their own experiences, interests and agendas.

Architectural education (and much of contemporary practice) is about brilliant individuals—solving a problem on his or her own terms. But in this case, no architecture student (and only one engineering student) participated in the entire process from beginning to end. The team had to design by committee. Surprisingly, the building is better because of this.

Trojan Goat

The team's design is a climate-responsive home that can adapt to a variety of weather conditions. Passive solar design, sustainable materials, as well as highly efficient mechanical, electrical and plumbing systems are essential components of the design. The house is powered entirely by photovoltaic cells. It has an energy storage system for use at night or on rainy days, and a control system to optimize the distribution of power efficiently.

The team attempted to creatively reuse discarded materials—reclaiming waste products before they entered a landfill or scrap yard. These included wooden shipping palettes; copper sheeting; automobile tires; even recently replaced stone pavers from the Rotunda building (designed by Thomas Jefferson), on the grounds of the university. Where reclaimed materials were not appropriate or available, the team used sustainable materials, to minimize the impact of the building on the environment.

The students designed and built all the cabinetry and most of the furniture in the house. The team also designed the surrounding landscape, including a grey water collection/filtration system, green roof, planters, decks, and garden. The landscape team grew many of the vegetables and other plants from seed, and harvested them during the event in Washington.

The house makes use of the first residential luminaire. Working with the Oak Ridge National Laboratory, a graduate architecture student assembled a domestic scale version of an emerging technology that provides natural daylight at locations far from a window. A mirror dish on the roof of the house tracks the sun, and concentrates it into a polished glass fiber cable to *deliver* the natural light directly into house's bathroom and entry hall.

Goats can easily adjust to seasonal and diurnal variations. They are said to be the most adaptable of mammals—able to adjust to any climate or terrain.

Early in the design process the house received a nickname that stuck. An architecture student was describing how a newly proposed sliding and hinging panels (similar to a rain screen wall) could form a climate responsive and protective skin around the entire building. Like a Trojan Horse, the building could arrive with a mysterious wrapper, and then unfold to reveal it's true intentions. Goats can easily adjust to seasonal and diurnal variations. They are said to be the most adaptable of mammals—able to adjust to any climate or terrain. They are also great recyclers—sometimes surviving on the waste of others. As the team discussed the Trojan Horse, it soon became the *Trojan Goat*.

Most importantly, the Trojan Goat identity clarifies the ethical framework of the design. The students decided they wanted the building to be ecologically responsible—not surprising given the brief of the competition—but on their own terms. It was to be adaptable, resourceful, intelligent, comfortable, highly evolved, but maybe a little rough around the edges. Refined, but handcrafted.

Process

During the design process, the team was assigned research and design activities to encourage effective collaboration. These included precedent analysis; domestic activity analysis; renewable energy research; a three week design / build project of a temporary winter sleeping shelter; and written progress reports to objectively assess the state of the design.

These activities were blended with more conventional architectural design phases—schematic design through construction drawings. Spread out over three full semesters, two partial semesters, and two summers, the team members often had to work with a loose understanding of the intentions of the students that preceded them in the project.

The difficulty of inter-disciplinary collaboration became a major source of both concern and inspiration. Engineers and architects speak different languages. On a basic level, there were differing expectations about what a house should be. Some engineering students could not see why the Trojan Goat wasn't more like a typical double-wide trailer which, if well insulated, could be very energy efficient.

Rather than attempt to completely redesign the house in response to these concerns, the later members of the architecture team became protective of both the building form and ethical principles behind it. They refined what the previous students had created. The schematic design employed a logical and well-proportioned ordering system, or module, which made the house both flexible and rigid. It allowed for refinement of the interior spaces and exterior skin without a complete rethinking of the building form.

A project management team established midway through the project helped the students and advisors streamline the decision-making process. Many complex issues were debated and resolved. They found a solution to balance a concern for energy efficiency with a desire for indoor-outdoor spatial continuity (i.e. full height glazing). In a series of difficult decisions, the team came up with a way to integrate mechanical and plumbing systems into the house that allowed for maximum efficiency but also clarified how the building works. In another internal debate that raged in passionate emails for several weeks, the team decided to accept a very limited use of pressure treated (arsenic) engineered lumber.

On the Mall and Beyond

Construction proceeded in fits and starts, but the house made it to Washington DC in time for the competition, and the UVA team fared well in the event—taking 1st Place in the architecture portion of the competition (design and livability) and 2nd Place overall. The team also tied for 1st Place in the Energy Balance category; was awarded a special citation from the American Institute of Architects; and received the BP Solar Progressive Award for the most forward-thinking team.

The architecture event was judged by a team of architects, including Australian Glenn Murcutt, who said:

> the design of solar homes must be as poetic as it is rational. The Virginia team fully considered building materials, insulation, ventilation and the use of light—whole building, sustainable design. There was little question that Virginia had the most inspired house.

According to jury chairwoman Stephanie Vierra,

> the UVA team attempted to integrate more solar strategies and did it more successfully than any other team. The work of the architecture and engineering students complemented each other in a way that set them apart from the other teams.

In a fitting tribute to the effective collaboration between the architecture and engineering parts of the UVA team, the Trojan Goat was the only house to place both in the top four of the architecture event and in the top four overall.

SOLAR HOUSE ON THE WEB:

http://www.faculty.virginia.edu/solarhome/

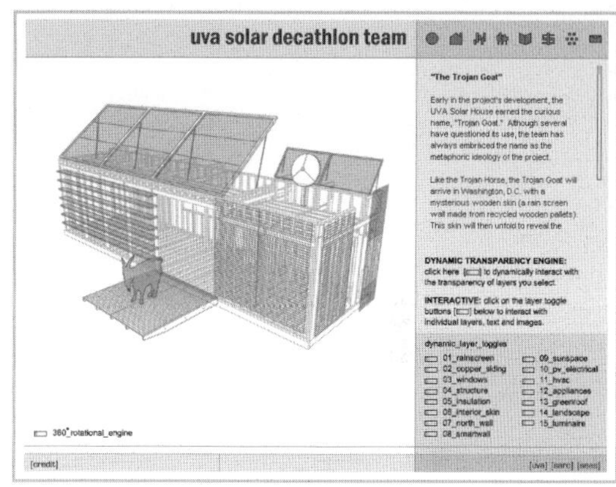

THE TROJAN GOAT IN THE PRESS:

"The University of Virginia team hand-crafted its long box as if it were a jewel, reshaping recycled materials as ordinary as wooden shipping pallets and as unusual as [bluestone] panels discarded from the terraces of Thomas Jefferson's alternative Rotunda."
Benjamin Forgery, architecture critic, Washington Post

"Taking 1st Place in design and 2nd Place in the entire competition was the University of Virginia entry, an intriguing modernist structure the size of a large mobile home framed in engineered wood and clad in reclaimed copper roofing. A distinctive system of louvers faced south to alternately deflect sunlight away from or reflect it into living spaces. Radiant-heat floors and valance cooling eliminated the need for forced-air-handling systems…"
Bradford McKee, Architecture Magazine

"The University of Virginia group won the design and livability category—which measured innovation and aesthetics—with sensuous copper-and-wood cladding, rooftop photovoltaics, and an elegant design. In devising a climate-responsive house, the team seized on the idea of a hard exterior unfolding to reveal a highly refined, nicely detailed interior. Recent graduate Teddy Nelson led the design of the building's exterior skin: copper siding from a collapsed barn roof shielded by an outer "rain screen" of reclaimed pallets and shipping-crate wood. The rain screen—operable louvers, window shutters, and movable shading devices—keeps out rain and high temperatures, creating an adjustable system that improves the efficiency of the house. Nelson says the students custom-built almost everything: 'We spent all summer hammering out copper and planing down pallet wood.'"
Kira L. Gould, Metropolis Magazine

306090 04 03 | 03

pp. 86-91 "Trojan Goat" ©2003 John Quale, Published by 306090, Inc.

Solar House web page screen shot ⟩

REMAKING WORLDS: THE MOBILE

We exist as points in the vastness
of the landscape, individuals in our
mobile pods of comfort...

The mobile studio satellite traveled 8,995 miles in search of America

STUDIO

by Linda Samuels

306090 04 03 | 03

©2003 Linda Samuels, Published by 306090, Inc.

pp. 92-101 "Mobile Studio"

Linda Samuels is an Assistant Professor of Architecture at the University of North Carolina at Charlotte, where she has been teaching for five years. Currently she teaches core design studios, and seminars in theory and photography. She holds degrees from the University of Florida and Princeton University. Her MArch at Princeton investigated the New Jersey Turnpike and fueled her interests in mobility, car culture and tourism.

In the spring of 2001 she began the development of the Mobile Studio as an experimental collaborative course. It was initiated in the Spring 2002 as a three-prong mobile curriculum of studio, seminar, and photography. The interdisciplinary studio traveled 8,995 miles, towing their custom-designed and student built trailer (The Mobile Studio Satellite) to collaborations with schools from around the USA.

Special Thanks: Rice University: Keith Krumweide, Stephen Fox, Lars Lerup. Arizona State University: Max Underwood. UNLV: Jose Gamez, Jeff Hartnett collaborators. Woodbury University: Jeanine Centuouri, tours by Gerry Smulevich and Jennifer Siegal. Thanks Also to: UNM: Gabriela Gutierrez, Tulane University: Scott Wall.

MAJOR SPONSORS: Graham Foundation for Advanced Studies in the Fine Arts, LEF Foundation, ACSA, University of North Carolina at Charlotte, UNCC College of Architecture

UNCC Student Participants: David Fish, Jedidiah Gant, Becky Joye, Couch Payne, Bill Sinkovic

contact: lcsamuel@email.uncc.edu

web: themobilestudio.org

1.ROADmap
interstate

42,000 mile National System of Interstate and Defense Highways—unified a system, and hence a population,  previously composed of scattered fragments. The public relations powers of politics and big business convinced the populace of a need for military security and high-speed individualized efficiency: the movement of troops, the landing of war planes, a "national interest", a race to be equal with the accomplishments of a nation on the verge of its own destruction. Interstates is also enterstates and innerstates. Made both possible and prominent the concept of the cross-country road trip, and the iconic literary versions of Kerouac's Dean Moriarty and cinematic, windblown easy riders—both embodying the simultaneous symbolic power of risk and destruction. With interstates came the new cowboy, the movie star, and the weekend warrior. Ultimately responsible, with help from technology, for the vast compression of time and space. Expanded the personal mobility radius from an average of 200 miles to 2000. Pulled "the farmer out of the mud." Infrastructure—a necessity of flow. An entirely new built typology: sculptural, sectional, expressive. **LINKS**

2.ROADmap
toll road

The planting of gates at the entrance to the great new public space. With options comes elitism, and the illusion of democracy enters the realm of mobility—separate, and not necessarily equal. Toll=ticket, ticket=entry. A restricted land comes with a different set of options—better maintenance, controlled services, greater support systems. Toll takes the price of expansion to the user rather than the general populace, allows the choice to pay rather than the requirement. The New Jersey Turnpike, the most famous of toll roads. Straightest road in the world, symbol of efficiency and expedience, has paid for itself over and over and yet continues to collect dimes and dollars from every driver. A  captive audience, a captured audience. A clearly defined entry and exit, an opportunity for marking, boundary, and identity. The toll of mobility—psychological as well as physical costs. **AMENITIES**

3.ROADmap
secondary

Opposite of interstate, microcosm versus macrocosm. Rural roads, small roads, slow roads. These roads link childhood houses to adulthood, neighbor to neighbor, memories. The Rural Studio in Hale County is a network of secondary roads, where experiments

Film Strip Images From The Mobile Studio "unitedinnerstates" by Jedidiah Gant

+ **Los Angeles, CA** is the jackpot of roads—in LA county, 92 million vehicle miles are driven every day on nearly 900 miles of high speed roadway. These roads are called names like "the 5" and "the 10" in true acceptance of their significance as objects. Yet, even though it is a city overwhelmed with driving and its infrastructure, it is a city that has accepted and integrated this system of high-speed sectional gymnastics into the landscape, both physical and psychological.

We are but tourists in our own homeland; we *go* but infrequently *know*. We are simultaneously obsessed and revolted by our love of movement and speed, finding it necessary to accomplish at a twenty-first century pace, finding it scarring to the landscapes of our lives. We comment on the beauty of the forests we drive through, but we glorify the tunnel of the road over the green itself, barely recognizing that the road we are on was once trees, too, and the green tunnel we are admiring would be all green without us to admire it. We consider accessibility an American birthright and immobility akin to death.

Americans in particular equate lack of movement with lack of progress, lack of growth, lack of success. We equate travel with culture (worldliness) and stationariness with backwardness. There is nothing worse for a writer than writer's block – being stuck, being still, hence being uncreative. Even those who stay painfully still (Annie Dillard, Sally Mann) study their surroundings microscopically so that the pace of their world is frenetic, requiring their own stillness as a datum of necessity. We are on the path to success, blood pumping through our veins, climbing the ladder, pounding the pavement, making our mark.

We photograph to document this movement, collect sites, own locations, make memories. We establish proof of our own successes through this collection of information. We are sure of it if we can hold it; the image is a tangible memory palace. Even better, we purchase the perfected memory palace of others, the souvenir postcard, and we send it out immediately so there is no mistaking progress for leisure. The private conquest merges with the institutionalized goal of the idealized view.

We exist as points in the vastness of the landscape, individuals in our mobile pods of comfort, joining each other in/on a community line as we come up to speed and eventually merge adjacent yet barely interactive with our mobile neighbors. This line weaves and pulses, converges and diverges, and eventually leaves the green hilly east and heads to flatness, aridity, mountains, hail, and rain. A trip west is associated with discovery, adventure, challenge. Photographers like Mathew Brady, Timothy O'Sullivan, and Ansel Adams shaped the idea of the western journey as they themselves saw the place for the very first time, then froze it and dispersed it as the iconographic understanding of the new frontier. Architects from Frank Lloyd Wright to Paolo Solari to Antoine Predock have built architectonic visions of the west and its specific palette of space and texture. It is a lifestyle captured on film and in literature, a *Thelma and Louise* parable of just keep going.

There exists a now standardized and dated two-sided mythology of mobility—on the one hand the destructive force that brought desolation and degradation to our urban cores, on the other a symbol of freedom, adventure, and progress. The first scenario is still rampant in the New South where cities like Atlanta, Georgia and Charlotte, North Carolina boast of sprawling growth that consumes over forty acres of forest and farmland every single day. California, however, stakes the largest claim on the second scenario. It is paradise, Oz, Hollywood; California is the final exit on the road to the American Dream. We have both created and inherited this environment that is a result of cultural obsessions. The city/suburb/exo-urb/megalopolis is a reification of the love/hate relationship Americans have with their automobiles.

306090 04 03 | 03

with materials and the necessities of living well are off of one and onto another. These are poorly maintained, gravel or dirt sometimes, they rest more lightly on the ground, are easier on bare feet and bicycle tires, but are rutted and rough on the cars that do make it. Often neglected, symbols of a barely mobile, and hence unworldly, uncivilized, and often unvalued area. Secondary, second class. A mix of mobility, slow and fast, car bike and pedestrian, people interacting with people at the pace of another time. (dirt road as representation of that other, pre-development time) textures and patterns—not paved in one solid black stroke—plaid roads, and striped roads. clean air, scenery, pace. A second look at the Rural Studio, a decade later. an ownership, a dignity, a patina not originally designed. sleeping spaces for storage, porch for storage, loft for storage. wallpaper of pictures. **SPEEDLESS**

4.ROADmap
controlled access

The myth of democracy. minimum and maximum speeds, the requirement of a car with a certain level of viability, a certain emission standard, a certain quality. Inspection due. What is a common language is also the language of control—exit only, merge, stay to the right, double lines. Required to be tagged and licensed to participate. Driving is a privilege, simultaneously registering you for the privilege to vote, to serve jury duty, and to be drafted for military service. You must be literate, in words and signs, you must maintain adequate vision, you must pull forward to pull back to park between two small orange cones. Self-control: no intoxication, no rage, no senility while moving at high speeds in the path of other multi-ton objects. stay in the lane. glaring and beeping in an attempt to control others. Control of the environment—serendipitous risk of the radio, or the microenvironment of a personal 5CD disk changer. temperature controls, window controls, seat controls. Surveillance, Jersey barriers placed at the entrances to all the Federal Buildings. No photos. The lack of a Federal building in Oklahoma City. Phoenix, Bruder's library, where the homeless are invited so that they might control the access that others have to them, and to their few possessions. **SELF**

5.ROADmap
service area

Consumption—"both an additive and subtractive process, both positive and negative, and both necessary and unnecessary." Distinguishing between a consumption of necessity and a consumption of desire. Desensitized through the mass media, the opportunity for transformation through the purchasing of our own value. Collecting—collecting places and memories, a set of state magnets, shell sculptures, postcards. Sharing place through this collecting. Welcome centers—the open arms at each state line. New Jersey Turnpike—where the service areas are named for famous

What might be considered the architecture of this mobile condition also often falls within these same two descriptions. The mobility myth is supported by an architecture of nostalgia or futurism (now also nostalgic), while the destructive side is evident at every interchange where acontextual monotony raises its consumerist flag. Though the latter is more insidiously omnipresent and inevitably more detrimental to the landscape, neither version brings the designer's potential relationship with mobility as a cultural and physical context into maturity.

In Edwin Abbott's book, *Flatland*, the geometric characters live in the restrictions of a table-top world—there is no *up*, only out. Mr. Sphere, the enlightened character from mysterious Space, attempts in vain to explain the third dimension to A. Square, the book's main character. Finally he resorts to ripping him from his comfortable two-dimensional life and yanking him into this Space where Mr. Square peers down and, exasperated, excited, and overwhelmed, proclaims the world an entirely fresh existence. There is no better way to see anew what surrounds you than to be pulled from mental and physical comfort, submerged in tactile experimentation, determinedly engaged in the search for a new vision.

Looking for new road maps.

pp. 92–101 "Mobile Studio" ©2003 Linda Samuels, Published by 306090, Inc.

Film Strip Images From The Mobile Studio "unitedinnerstates" by Jedidiah Gant

+ **Houston, TX** and its sculptural flying highways and non-existent zoning (and hence highly variable physical context), known as the city with the largest land mass metro area due to its overzealous annexation policies. A place founded on piney woods, prairie, marsh, ship channels, ports, and bayous that has emerged, drought ridden or flooding, in a nonhierarchical spread into the wet heat of east Texas.

Alternative Pedagogical Models and an Attempt to Discover a New Reality

You want to do what?

Driving that Ford Expedition, towing that 6,000 pound trailer, was like driving a speedboat pulling a herd of buffalo. Week one was the most difficult, as we bounced our way down 85 South, through spaghetti junction and into rural Alabama. The foliage and the landscape weren't new to us yet, and the constant saltine sawdust, abandoned reading materials, and headphone isolation nearly halted this adventure before it even started. Though the satellite held the studio and the darkroom with all their accompanying supplies (and all our luggage), the Expedition was loaded with the 6 of us, 3 laptops, 8 cameras, 2 video cameras, pillows, winter coats, CD players, nearly 600 CDs, batteries, snacks, sketchbooks, maps, random shoes and socks, and a partially depleted first aid kit. After planning for over a year and a half, on the morning of February 15th 2002 we finally pulled out of the construction yard of the UNCC College of Architecture and onto the road that would lead us to the larger road system that would eventually lead us across this country. I had never driven an SUV or anything like it, and I certainly had never pulled even the smallest of trailers. That first day was shaky and swerving and scary for all of us, and it

seems we went at least a week without attempting to go in reverse. It wasn't really until we crossed the Mississippi River, drove through Louisiana swamp country and toward Texas, that I felt we were truly on the road.

In traditional design school terminology, The Mobile Studio might be considered an extended field study, a design/build project, and an inter-disciplinary collaboration, but there is no traditional terminology that explains what one might gain from spending 8 weeks driving 9,000 miles across Americas a group of 5 students and one professor. The initial mission—to focus on a contemporary vision of the road was never distinct from its methodology—to be submerged, immersed, and entirely focused by being in it, on it, and looking at it at all times. This immersion technique had three simultaneous tracks: design (studio), history (pop culture)/ theory (seminar), and a visual track (photography), encouraging thorough and intense stare by which new discoveries would inevitably be made. By investigating The Mobile Studio as an example of an alternative pedagogical model, we might begin to understand how this and other alternatives to the traditional studio/seminar format might inspire both the professional and academic *imagining* and *remaking.*

From Inside the Tank
(The Satellite as a Frame for Experience)

The concept behind the exploration was to be an on-site, in-depth roving design laboratory—an extended arm of our parent institution linked to the College of Architecture and the larger design world via the technological umbilical cords of modern communication. Two factors were key to the success of this premise—places to land (sites and people of collaboration) and a physical framework to support our mission. The Mobile Studio Satellite (MSS) is that framework, the vehicle—both literally and figuratively—designed as a base for creative operations while on the road. A 6,000 pound custom trailer, the MSS was designed and built over the fall semester of 2001 and the month prior to departure. Its objective is to integrate the complementary components of the curriculum in three primary ways: collecting, creating, and communicating. Each component of the MSS—light-tight box, spine, cavity, and shell—contributes in a variety of ways to this objective.

Collecting is both physical and visual, a process of exploring and a process of seeing. The light-tight box operates as a pinhole camera and photographic darkroom, freezing in the most rudimentary (yet educational) way the sites and situations encountered. The spine is the technical

people who were from New Jersey, or lived in New Jersey, or happened to drive through while someone was paying attention. Accessible, efficient, and reliable (redundant) without having to exit the gates of this self-contained world. Another new typology, the combination of previously disparate services for the sake of expedience—refuel, relieve, revive. Occasionally, havens for alternative forms of experience—sex, drugs, crime. Opportunities for a captive audience—education, recreation, orientation, community. A chance to develop pace and identity along the road, to mark progress and set goals. Las Vegas as the ultimate service area—an entire economy devoted to the fantasies of its paying customers. **PAUSE.**

6.ROADmap
national monument

Brown signs marking places designated by governing bodies as significant. A country-wide history from the scale of the plaque to the tower. A network of relevant and cumulative points of interest. History is interpretive; significances change, and disappear. There is a map of places, natural and beautiful, and a map of ideas. Memorials. Sacred ground. Place as monumental, ideas as monumental. Maya Lin's civil rights memorial is the object, but the place is that road that runs through Selma, and the idea is long-overdue equality. Roads as monuments. The road that jazz took to get to New Orleans, and the aura of the era of Route 66. The non-monument: statistical highs and lows (the lowest elevation in the 48 contiguous states), the beautifully kitschy (south of the border, cadillac ranch), the middle of nowhere, Roswell New Mexico. Preserved urbanity. **MEMORY**

7.ROADmap
attraction

Las Vegas - the attraction of one's own vices. The ultimate smorgasbord of choices, where attraction itself is the root of the economy. "The water problem here is a myth. Water runs towards money." The fastest growing city in America; the number one tourist destination in the entire world. And an infinite pool of work for those who want it. Hope as an attraction, starting over, success and stability through honest labor that serves the building of infinite fantasies. An oasis in the desert. An influx of retirees, flocking to the tax-free desert heat, the plethora of gated communities, and the desire to be surrounded by the security of homogeneity. Moving higher and higher up the hill for the view, frequently shrouded with the dust of growth. In this case the importation of culture as an attraction—the new Rem Vegas Guggenheim, the previously controversial Gehry motorcycle show, the mini-Eiffel. In Houston, culture is a real attraction, with a matriarch brilliant enough to prioritize quality in the works, and the works that house them. **CULTURE.**

7.ROADmap
boundary

Making the sound of a pretend rifle shot at the crossing of every state line—a celebration, a mark of achievement, progress. Thirteen states, and Texas four times. These are marked by signs, mottos, pseudo-vernacular huts of orientation and consumerism. The real boundary is the southern one—marked by chain link fence with barbed wire, a deep pit of murky water, and men with guns.

306090 04 03 | 03

pp. 92-101 "Mobile Studio" ©2003 Linda Samuels, Published by 306090, Inc.

Film Strip Images From The Mobile Studio"unitedinnerstates" by Jedidiah Gant

+ **Las Vegas, NV** is the fastest growing city in America and the number one tourist destination in the entire world, surpassing Mecca for that honor in the year 2000. It is a city built entirely around a single road, the famous Las Vegas Strip, and a single idea, the selling of a fantasy experience. Yet it is trapped mobility, anti-mobility – the roadside moves faster than the road itself.

zone, storing collected data; at its base is the solar battery system, collecting the energy of the sun. The shell acts as a curio cabinet, a vessel first empty then gradually filled with the collected relics of the journey. The collection itself becomes a mark of distance, a measure of progress both physical and conceptual.

Creating occurs within the cavity, a studio-based space devoted to both individual and group activities of analysis, process, and design. In the cavity are two sliding drafting boards, six flat-files, a model-building station, and large storage compartments for raw materials. The spine organizes and supports the cavity, becoming a technological brain for creative activity as well as a source for power and lighting.

Communicating happens continuously along the line of movement and strategically at the points of pause. The shell constantly communicates the Mobile Studio's identity, mission, and progress. As the curio cabinet fills, the translucency shifts towards opacity as our creative projects transform the shell of the MSS from a framework of raw materials to a display space of creative work. The chalkboard surface on the front of the Satellite tallies mileage, locations, and days.

The success of the MSS was multi-fold. First, as the product of fund-raising, design collaboration and group construction, it operated prior to the semester as a symbol of faith and commitment—of the students preparing for the experimental journey, but also of the design world outside of our immediate sphere. Daily, it functioned as a reification of our missions—literal immersion in and celebration of mobility; the integration of the curricular tracks, the generation and reinforcement of our larger identity, the *advertising* of not only our agenda but our progress towards that agenda through the diminishing transparency and hence completion of design work along the way.

It is this considerable presence, however, that also made us extremely IMMOBILE at times—the MSS weighs nearly 6,000 pounds, reaches 7'-6" high and is actually constructed more like a tank than a trailer. In essence, we were immediately removed from *normal* mobility issues by virtue of physical presence. Optimistically, this also contributed to our hyper-consciousness—every move was exaggerated, every driving decision more careful and more critically planned than the typical maneuvering of the personal vehicle.

With this nomadic identity came the rules and language (and also the opportunities) of a mobile life.

A Moving Vision
(Accepting Nomadism as a Frame of Reference)

At the temporal halfway point, the significant difference between short-term mobility (traveling, commuting, daily living) and long-term mobility (itinerant, peripatetic, adventurous, homeless, wanderer) became glaringly obvious. After four weeks on the road, we recognized our own situation as more nomadic than touristic. The MSS, the vehicle, and the six of us created a homeland microcosm whose stable, recurring context was the gas station, the quick mart, and the road. Here, a relieving, refueling, observing and note-taking ritual occurred every three hours. Headphones and portable CD players worked as space makers, providing privacy and an opportunity for individual introspection in a space barely 9x6 feet.

With this nomadic identity came the rules and language (and also the opportunities) of a mobile life. The language is one of signs—boundaries, exits, sites, pauses, limits—and symbols—blinkers, double lines, license plates, bumper stickers, arrows. The defining of space at this pace is relative—the flatness of this versus what came before it, the brown of this landscape versus the previous green. Every feature is a piece of an ever-growing comparison, and every mile an opportunity to be somewhere new. Road time is not the same as

Crossed by accident, no U-turns allowed, and the line—hundreds of cars long—to get into the United States is at a standstill. It is a boundary of opportunity, and of home. You can see the bronze eagle, the American flag, and the golden arches from the line. Personal space boundaries—made in a packed car with limited supplies—a differentiation between light areas and dark, middle seat and back, headphones and cd players as a way to make privacy. Or sleep. A nomadic life, rules inside the car are different than the rules of a stationary existence. Road rules. Mobility attempts to separate you from your stationary existence, but technology breaks those boundaries—the CD player imports home into the car, the cell phone allows the intrusion of responsibility at will. The group is limited, in or out, boundaries of acceptance, boundaries of behavior. *IDENTITY.*

8.ROADmap
time zone

Road time is not the same as city time. Road time is measured in caffeine intake (and output), gas stops, miles per gallon. It is exit numbers, not second hands. And it is different going east than west. Going west you are beating the clock, gaining time, chasing the sun. You can lose three hours in a day going east if you happen to drive on the edge of daylight savings time. Driving cross-country you exist in all time zones—home, last stop, this stop, next stop. The edge of the time zone is when the cell phone display magically changes, or you reset the laptop. The noticeable changes, though, are the ones between interstates and secondary roads, the places where time has taken over next to the places that time forgot. Nostalgia is preservation. Las Vegas is its own time zone, 24 hours a day of activity and stopped dead traffic. Los Angeles has three time zones—morning rush hour, afternoon rush hour, and the blur of time for those who don't bother with commuting—or with working. The cycle of rituals, the rotating of tires, the changing of oil. The visual zones are in the landscape—the plush weedy green that runs from North Carolina to northern Louisiana, the wide open landscape across Texas and the southwest, the hilly and fragrant southern California spring. Visual, sensual, defining. **SHIFTS.**

9.ROADmap
scenic route

An intense combination of beauty and nausea, antithetical to the original intentions of high-speed mobility, more a compromise between driving and walking. The windshield as a frame, bringing the imprecise beauty of nature to the very edge of the big metal beast. The scenic route is even further sterilized by the safety-driven pull off and the commercially obnoxious Kodak spot. More an attempt to duplicate than to create, the Kodak spot removes the

306090 04 03 | 03

pp. 92–101 "Mobile Studio" ©2003 Linda Samuels, Published by 306090, Inc.

Civil Rights Bridge by Bill Sinkovic

+ **Phoenix, AZ** in a sublimely beautiful landscape with a 180 degree horizon, the second-fastest growing city in the country, now a multi-nodal megalopolis reinvented from rugged Mexican frontier to "elderly white-haired ghetto" in less than 40 years thanks to the mastermind developers of a place called Sun City and the widespread availability of a necessity called air-conditioning.

stationary time. Road time is measured in caffeine intake (and output), gas stops, miles per gallon, exit signs. Road time is different going east than going west. Going west you are beating the clock, gaining time, chasing the sun.

Mobility attempts to separate you from your stationary existence, but guarded by a fear of that loss, technology breaks those boundaries. The CD player imports home into the car and removes the risk of the randomness and even emptiness of the dial; the cell phone allows the intrusion of responsibility at will and insures that comforts of work and home are within our *no roaming and no long distance* plans. These tethers and their additional nearly-instantaneous extension of email are both advantages and disadvantages. On the one hand, they minimize the sense of freedom and tangibly resist leaving home (and all it represents) behind; on the other, they allow a thread of that previous existence to remain, and particularly in this condition based on progress and academic achievement, they allow scheduling to occur and communication to remain open.

A Unified Vision
(Advantages of an Integrated Curriculum)

The collection of Mobile Studio work—Satellite, research, design projects, photographs, writing, video, website—presents its own two-sided dilemma. On the one hand it makes you continually alert, alive, and curious where, by necessity, you are always reinventing, adjusting, solving problems, and testing the limits of your adaptability; on the other side, the much less significant side, it is exhausting. This brings up infinite pedagogical questions: In a round-the-clock academic life, how do you balance class with no class? Focus with distraction? Targeted knowledge with knowledge gained through osmosis? Together with apart? Routine with adventure? What is a 24-hour-a-day mobile methodology?

Each participant in The Mobile Studio returned home changed in some way—more worldly, more socially conscious, more determined, more confident, more tolerant. These changes are results of wide open eyes and random requests off the map as much as results of the structured curriculum and planned collaborations. The human element was the most surprising, like eating fried catfish down the street from the Rural Studio Butterfly house, or serendipitously crossing paths with the fabulous and friendly Cowboy Poets on our way to Marfa, or

306090 04 03 | 03

pp. 92-101 "Mobile Studio" ©2003 Linda Samuels, Published by 306090, Inc.

Film Strip Images From The Mobile Studio
by Jedidiah Gant

control of visual variables from the photographer and attempts to limit the creativity of image-making. The most scenic routes are in the places that look entirely unlike where you are from. Rural west Texas, southern Arizona, and northern New Mexico show off 180 degrees of horizon and a monstrous dome of sky. Magritte clouds. James Turrell is moving tons of earth over years of work in an attempt to frame this sky and make it visible. **SENSES.**

10.ROADmap
park

Ease of parking is taken for granted. The average pre-SUV car fits easily in any standard parking space, goes in both forward and reverse with ease, and maintains full use of all glass areas including windows and mirrors. A trailer does the very unintuitive act when going in reverse of turning in the opposite direction of the vehicle that is towing it. Pull-through spaces and unlined dirt lots deserve a level of respect for their unobtrusiveness. Mastered vehicle weight=driver empowerment. The wide-open road is the most fully accessible and uncrowded of all the parks in the National system. At the right time of year, there is easy visual access to unadulterated landscape. The greatest of these roads literally runs through the actual parks, creating in essence a drive-thru version of nature. **POWER.**

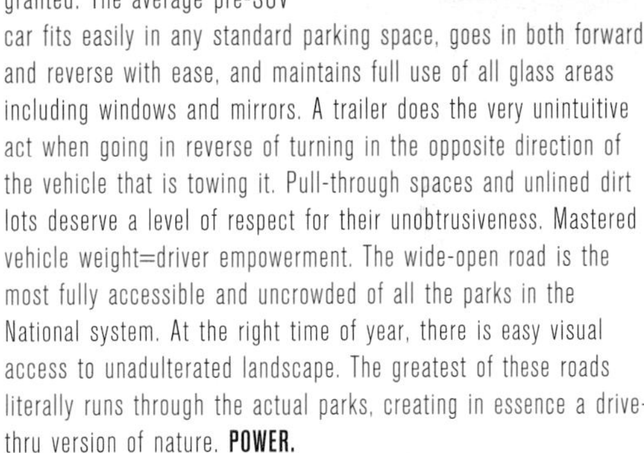

11.ROADmap
under construction

Evolution. Destruction. Rebirth. Access and exit ramps are suspended, cantilevered into space with rebar tentacles reaching into the void. It is uncertain if these are ruins or progress. They stay in that condition seemingly for months, and then the gap is closed and this new road is now crucial to existence. The typology of the on-ramp is a case study in sculptural prowess. They are the near structurally pure combination of compression and tension in reinforced concrete, formed from the malleable mix of this pourable material. They express an identity of place through their material color, emblems or symbols, construction techniques, and formal qualities. Houston's highways are supported on orchard-like columns, flying through the air in a complexity of section; the highways of the desert rest mostly on the ground, glowing the yellowish tint of native sand. Construction is both a contribution and a detractor to the goals of mobility. It is often intended to allow an increase in traffic volume, but rarely does. Its strength is repair—smooth, even, fast. **PROGRESS.**

the very real memorial for the victims of September 11th, set up at the base of the very unreal New York New York Las Vegas hotel. We read *On the Road* and *Travels with Charlie* and watched *Easy Rider* and *Thelma and Louise*, but in the end the trip was more Partridge Family than Kerouac, and we made our own order out of the universal language of the road and the variety of our personalities.

Speaking at SCI-Arc during our visit, James Turrell described Rodencrater, a cosmic hole in the desert he is slowly transforming into a monstrous artwork. His goal is to move thousands of tons of earth to the exact right location to frame the sky. This, in some ways, could be a metaphor for the mission of The Mobile Studio. For every driver and passenger who saw us on the road, every student and faculty member we collaborated with, every group we presented our work to, we succeeded in making the invisible visible. Our original focus was mobility, but our larger mission became awareness. Awareness of mobility, yes, (which has redefined itself for us at every collaboration) but also awareness of education and architecture as *active* rather than passive pursuits. Each person's ability to contribute or exist in this design world is improved exponentially by a broadening of vision, and for each participant, this adventure also demanded a greater investigation of personal identity and an examined ethic about how one mediates between themselves and the world.

SPECULATE MEDIATE

LANDSCAPE AS CONTESTED IDEAL

In June 2002, CNN reported that for the first time, the world urban population surpassed the world rural population. The concept of landscape as retreat or as otherwise distanced from urban anxiousness and the disorder becomes impossible. Out there is no longer there. Everything and all other remote places are now in the city. Infrastructure becomes the new global topography. Cemeteries with acres of *nothing* become culturally excessive in all the right real-estate ways. And the productive landscape escalates into nostalgic marketing—a pastoralization of the skyscraper. Given this context, *Landscape* as a term, defies traditional boundaries. Its organizational efficacy diminishes as our understanding of it gains intensity and degrees of separation become surgical. Under scrutiny, Landscape explodes beyond limited notions of *green* into thick strategies of continuity and spatial identity. Whether physical systems, economic networks, historical agendas or social and cultural manifestations of the everyday, Landscape is the connective tissue of our environment. Its role as both adjective and verb triumphs over noun.

Landscapes, as reconsidered in this body of work, are a result of complex negotiations between intellectual constructs and physical space. Made evident through outlines on maps, astronomical lines, cultural diversions, points of exchange, political territories, and economic shifts, they are anything but unilateral. Rather, landscapes call into question the differences and continuities that take place from one point to another, transforming a seemingly neutral space to a complex and contested terrain. The notion of a landscape as site of negotiation assumes a condition of flux whereby the programmatic, spatial or cultural definition of a space is pinned only momentarily to ever-changing framework. It is through the intensification of the limits of this framework that liminal landscapes emerge, caught somewhere between abstraction and reality, cause and effect. The conditions which define landscapes are always understood relative to these negotiations, offering a multitude of ways by which to explore the implications for design.

Issues studied by the studios ranged in scale and specificity, from cultural critique to site revitalization. Programmatic options included the vitality of urban landscape and infrastructure, the contemplative landscape of death, and changing modes of production in the rural landscape.

Students at the University of Michigan explore liminal landscapes

ACTIVATE:

by Elise Shelley, Gretchen Wilkins and Neal Robinson

The works documented herein are part of a larger "Landscape" design studio collective whose efforts were initiated by Architecture program chair, Tom Buresh and with financial support from Leon Reiskin, BArch '51. The studios were instructed by six faculty members at the Taubman College of Architecture + Urban Planning: Kevin Benham, Caroline Constant, Coleman Jordan, Neal Robinson, Elise Shelley and Gretchen Wilkins.

Elise Shelley is a Lecturer in Architecture at the University of Michigan. She is a graduate of the University of Virginia, with degrees in both architecture and landscape architecture. She is a registered landscape architect and has ongoing projects in Ontario, Michigan and Massachusetts.

Gretchen Wilkins is currently a Lecturer at the Taubman College of Architecture and Urban Planning at the University of Michigan. She is a graduate of the University of Michigan and a founding partner of SOMA Design in Ann Arbor with John Comazzi.

Neal Robinson is a Lecturer in Architecture at the University of Michigan. A graduate of Rice University, he is a registered architect and founding partner of WETSU in Ann Arbor, Michigan. From 1998 to 2000, he was the sole proprietor of SKYlab architectures in Atlanta, Georgia.

The projects illustrated here were completed by architecture students in their second semester of the two-year professional degree program at the University of Michigan.

Shelley Studio Participants:
Evrensel Atila, Joanne Behrens, Hackjong Choi, Gina Cicero, Scott Floria, Christopher Hillegas, George Konidis, Timothy Lago, Pedro Melis, Kevin Myshock, Merlinda Song, Robert Webber, Mert Yilmaz

Wilkins Studio Participants:
Mican Andrews, Kourtney Baldwin, Beth Cady, Shannon Easter, Keith Manuel, Jaimelyn Manipula, Randy Moreland, Holly Osterhout, Youngsup Park, Mark Redden, Nubras Samayeen, Sunphol Sorakul, Matthew Stark

Robinson studio participants:
Ahn Dongjoon, So Eun Cho, Lorell Comulada-Cruz, Gideon Danilowitz, Yuntaek Hyun, Jeong Han Kim, Kyong-Hee Kim, Sang-Beom Kim, Lui-Shun Lau, Amy Milobowski, Yoo Chul Roe, Amanda Spicuzzi, Benjamin Yonce

306090 04 03 03

Published by 306090, Inc.

pp. 102-109 "Speculate Mediate Activate" ©2003 Elise Shelley et al,

Background Image: Lorell Comulada

Overhead / Underground
A Study of Landscape and Infrastructure in Toronto, Canada

In the urban realm, landscape is often rendered illegible by the density of the built fabric and infrastructure has lost its role as an integral component of civic form. This studio explored the concept of infrastructure as a structurally significant component of the city, capable of contributing aesthetically, spatially and functionally to the urban landscape.

The meaning of infrastructure has broadened significantly from its original reference to engineered structures and systems at a local scale, to a global understanding of built or virtual networks. Historically, infrastructure consisted of public works—urban structures and landscapes operating at the civic scale—that contributed to urban vitality. Then, as now, the design of such systems consciously incorporated multiple functions and scales, integrating regional needs with local networks, thus imbuing public spaces and landscapes with cultural significance. Yet today the density and monolithic zoning of modern cities either renders infrastructure invisible or compromises its role in the public imagination as an integral component of civic form. This studio proposed to recover the concept of infrastructure as both functional landscape and civic gesture, capable of contributing to the aesthetic and spatial renewal of the broader urban landscape.

To understand the diminishing aesthetic value of civic infrastructure, students examined the history of Toronto, where the increasing scale of infrastructure has fragmented the urban core. Over the last hundred years, the city's downtown core has become isolated both physically and visually from its harbor on Lake Ontario. This isolation resulted from the advent of large-scale transportation networks serving sea, rail and automobile transport. The nega-tive impact of inland rail and water transportation systems, originally developed to serve the shipping industry, was exacerbated by the addition of regional arteries oriented toward automobile and truck traffic. Rather than being perceived as civic infrastructure, these new systems formed barriers that truncate streets, isolate green spaces and restrict pedestrian movement. The functional logic of civic infrastructure leads to a negative understanding of infrastructure, diminishing its capacity to operate as a positive component of urban form.

This studio looked to the urban condition of Toronto, to propose infrastructure as a potential manifestation of landscape within the city. Public works were investigated at various scales to reconfigure the relationship of the city to its harbor and to recover the potential of new networks to operate as civic infrastructure.

The accommodation of local activities and public services are simultaneously addressed by interventions that reorganize existing systems at the urban scale to reestablish Toronto's harbor front as an integral part of the metropolitan core.

Design projects incorporating analysis of urban conditions, city-scale conceptualizations, and human-scale interventions redefined notions of landscape, its role in the city, and the relationships formed by infrastructural systems.

Elise Shelley

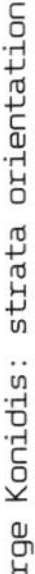

TOPOGRAPHIC SYSTEMS

Early studies of Toronto's topography and geologic history allowed projects to manipulate landform and create new spatial conditions. The city's history of engineered landfills along the waterfront suggested the malleability of earthwork and the potential to use ground as a medium for construction.

Strata Orientation [opposite]

By dispersing a system of prototypical vertical light-shafts throughout the downtown core George Konidis's proposal creates an identifiable system of connection and orientation.

The studio explored the concept of infrastructure as a structurally significant component of the city.

HYDROLOGIC SYSTEMS

The hydrological conditions of Toronto's glacial landscape sculpted a system of ravines that stitch various urban neighborhoods to the harbor. At the same time the harbor front has been repeatedly reconfigured by urban infrastructure serving the shipping industry. Projects sought to link the natural systems and the engineered systems by using this topographic anomaly as a point of departure.

Dynamic Interface [left]

Joanne Behrens's project extends Toronto's harbor inward to negotiate the isolation of the urban core from the water's edge. A zippered interlock of programs, buildings and public spaces integrates land and water activities, creating an expanded edge condition to prompt redevelopment and revitalization of the harbor.

MOVEMENT SYSTEMS

Toronto's urban core is the hub of an extensive regional transportation system that serves pedestrians and vehicles both above and below ground. The complexity of existing movement systems suggests a need for reorientation and reconnection of infrastructures to rationalize movement networks throughout the city.

(Sub) way-finding [left - middle]

To alleviate the disorienting effects of being submerged in Toronto's underground system, Merlinda Song's project introduces a new type of distribution center that focuses on the retrieval and dispersal of information within this circulation zone.

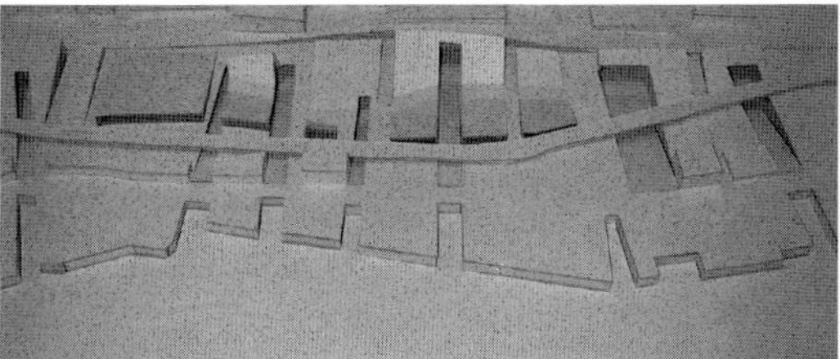

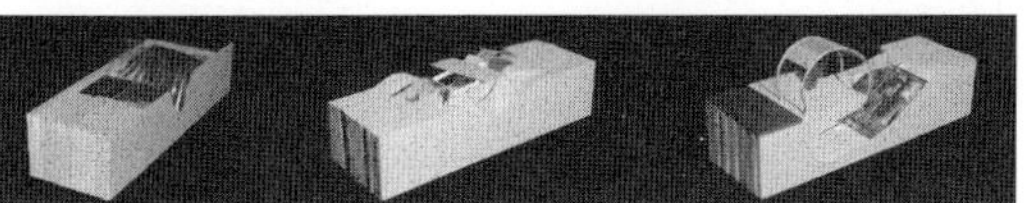

306090 04 03 | 03

pp. 102-109 "Speculate Mediate Activate" ©2003 Elise Shelley et al, Published by 306090, Inc.

Images by Joanne Behrens [top], Merlinda Song [middle], Pedro Melis [bottom]

"Death is a transition; but it is only the last in a long chain of transitions. The moment of death is related not only to the process of afterlife, but also to the process of living, aging, and producing progeny. Death relates to life: to the recent life of the deceased and to the life he or she has procreated and now leaves behind. Life continues generation after generation, and in many societies it is this continuity that is focused on and enhanced during the rituals surrounding a death. The continuity of the living is a more palpable reality than the continuity of the dead. Consequently it is common for life values and fertility to dominate the symbolism of death rituals." [1]

Rituals surrounding death and dying are embedded in understandings of landscape—be they cultural, religious, geographic or architectural. The mythologies that inform everyday life are inseparable from those of death. Similarly, the way the dead are treated reflects cultural, social and religious beliefs in life and afterlife. If architecture can be understood as a participant in the rituals of death, landscape is the site that embodies and facilitates those rituals. Together they comprise a ritual landscape, which reflects the traditions, programs and issues inherent to death while serving the collective body of the living.

This studio focused on death and dying, from the physical body to the urban landscape. At the root of these explorations was an analysis and redefinition of rituals of death relative to commercial, industrial, urban or other institutional values. Each student researched various cultural and religious attitudes toward death and interpreted them for a site within a particular American cultural and historical context—the post-industrial landscape of Detroit.

The site is the former location of the Jeffries Homes West, a housing project built in Detroit during the 1950s to house immigrant auto workers. Of the original thirteen towers, only four remain. Three have been renovated and the fourth is slated for demolition. This site—chosen for its complex history, current evacuated condition, diverse boundaries and urban adjacencies—suggests multiple opportunities for intervention relative to the student research.

To address this site, the students confronted the American infrastructure of death—those public and commercial industries that provide services for the public upon the event of death. These industries—which include cemeteries, crematories, morticians, florists, musicians, et cetera—provide what is conventionally known as the "necessary" arrangements that

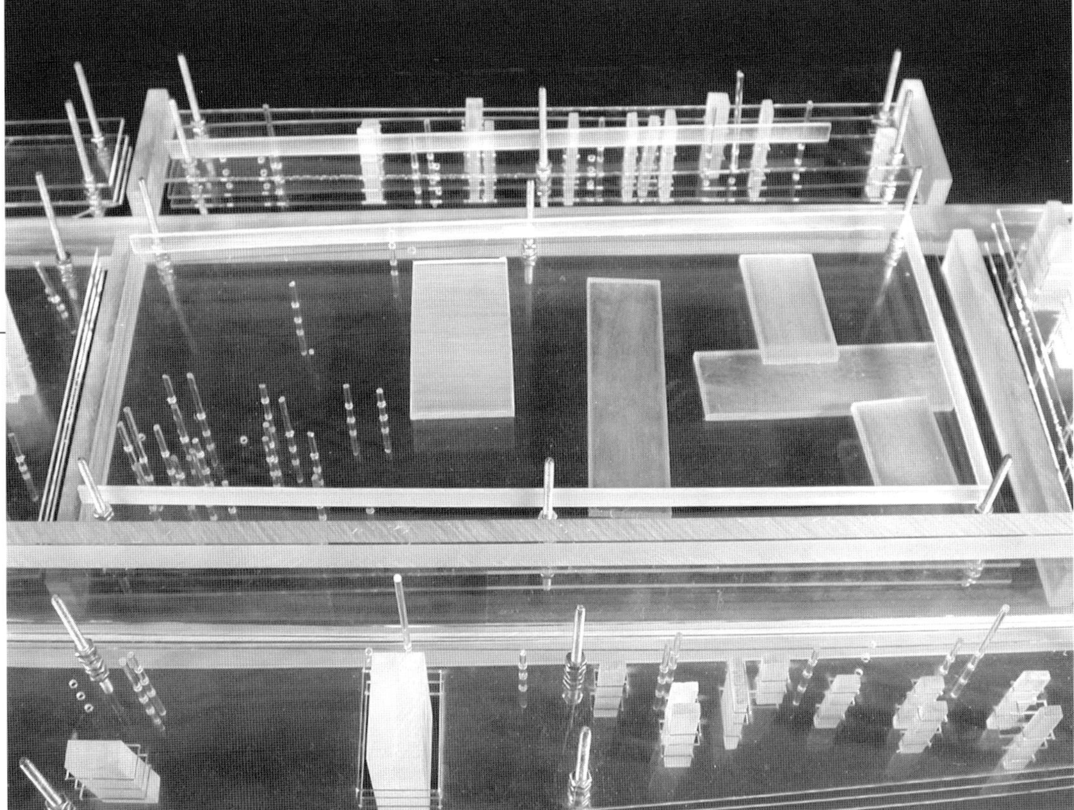

Rituals surrounding death and dying are embedded in understandings of landscape—be they cultural, religious, geographic or architectural

enable the orchestrated public events that make up commercial America's death rituals. These public events may not be limited to the ceremony and the wake, but can also occur at the scale of "necro-tourism" in cemeteries such as Père-Lachaise in Paris (which statistically contains the greatest number of famous people per square mile and is visited by two million tourists each year), Mt. Auburn in Cambridge or the necropolises of Pompeii, Herculaneum and ancient Rome. In these cases life and death do not oppose one another, but instead work to blur the historic distinctions between metropolis and necropolis, museum and mausoleum. The work in this studio challenges the program of death by engaging the site's cultural, historical and architectural potential, resulting in projects that deal with death physically and/or socially in the urban realm. Death is not understood solely as a point of finality or absence, but equally as an occasion for leisure, learning and/or remembrance.

Gretchen Wilkins

End Notes:

[1] Richard Huntington and Peter Metcalf, "Celebrations of Death: An Anthropology of Mortuary Ritual" (Cambridge: Cambridge University Press, 1979) p 93.

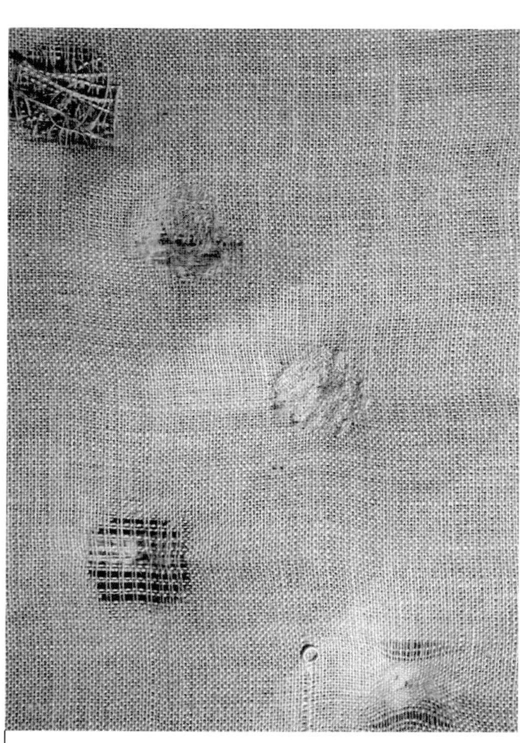

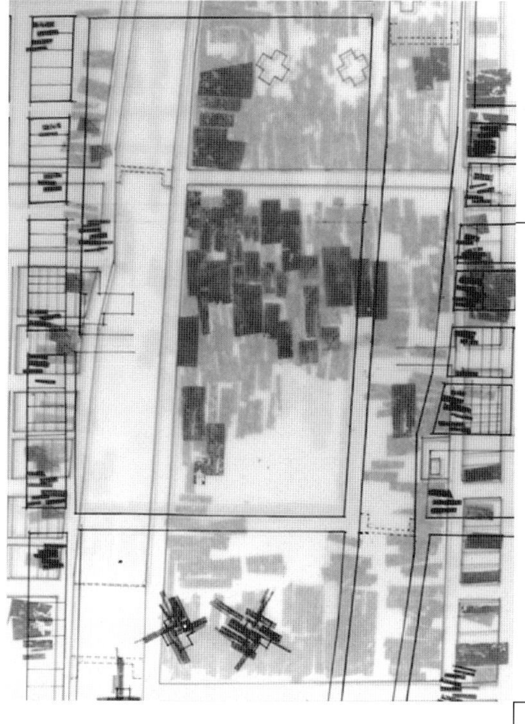

Matthew Stark: site momentum [left]
Nubras Samayeen [right]

306090 04 03|03

©2003 Elise Shelley et al, Published by 306090, Inc.

pp. 102-109 "Speculate Mediate Activate"

Hatching Landscape

To "hatch" a landscape implies both procedural
attentiveness through nurturing and prolonged
maintenance, as well as a way of calling to
our attention a graphic or situational poche—a
difference from the normal surroundings. It is these
two dispositions—the process and the inscription,
which reveal the fundamentals of cultivating a
landscape. Much like the farmer whose marking
of the land with a mechanical plow is inseparable
from the act of divining the sky, vision and visions
conspire to produce the world as we (want to) know
it. To separate landscape from architecture or nature
from man is to embark on an exquisitely heretical
path. Making these distinctions locally, for oneself, is
to ultimately implicate the body of us all on a more
global scale. This is not to intimidate of course, but
to implicate our thoughts as demonstrative actions.
Through characterization, disposition and free will,
the most effective grounding implements are forged.

On our path to becoming lunatics, this studio
explored the thoughtful grounding of an architecture
by interrogating both landskip, the appropriation
of landscape a pictorial, potentially distancing
operation, and landschaft, the understanding
of landscape as a series of intimate territorial
relationships that facilitate patterns of occupation
and use. In short, we exploited the (unfair?)
characterization of the urban view of landscape in
relation to the seemingly productive situation of
the rural farmer. For us to imagine landscape as
out there is to promote the pictorial. It directs the
understanding of landscape not to a singular focus
or object, but to an overall scenic totality. Sight itself
becomes the object of awareness. This separates
landscape from its explicitly useful qualities and
isolates it as merely an intellectual endeavor. As
Jorgen Des argues:

*When landscape comes into aesthetic honor
and dignity as a symbolic representation
of nature as a whole, it is not within the
perspective of the farm worker. The aesthetic
enjoyment of nature is a privilege for the
bourgeois individual, who is removed from
nature in his everyday life. When we disregard
the farm worker, landscape doesn't relate to our
existence.*[1]

With the realization that as a part of our current
cultural situation, theoria, or the essential
connectivity and understandability of things has
been set adrift. Most students responded with
certain distancing from the pictorial—both in
ideology and in representation. Landschaft was
favored over landskip. They embraced the notion
that while landscape is indeed tied to vision; it
is more importantly linked to physical reality—a
state of existence that seems to scientifically and
culturally evaporate as quickly as it condenses.
Because this *reality* is in continuous flux, so is the
unity of landscape. Thus, to farm or cultivate design
strategies, the studio adopted a position wherein
the unique was no longer privileged as the point
of departure. Instead, the *unique* was transferred
to the individual methodologies or processes of
construction of that reality—a produced landscape.

The agents for the productive landscape were
the program—a hatchery for producing and
manufacturing fish. And secondly, the constructed
mythology of/or the pseudo-science of fly-fishing.
The site was the physical limits of Gallup Park—a
pastoral construction of Ann Arbor, Michigan's
Parks and Recreation Department. It is deliberately
un-urban in character. The overlay of the studio
sets up potential conflicts of ideology, usability and
physical scale.

Making distinctions locally, for one-self, is to ultimately implicate the body of us all on a more global scale.

Fly-fishing, a popular recreational sport in *the land of 10,000 lakes*, together with it's mix of unapologetic dependency on intuition provided the analogous mythos for our thinking about landscape and it's potential liberation from *not architecture*. Students began by investigating perhaps the most iconic representation of the sport fishing landscape—the fishing fly. Each chose a fly, or pairs of flies based on it's ability to lure either someone or something—a visual vs. informational decision. Upon returning to studio, the students analyzed their finds, and perhaps more importantly the circumstances of their selection, both graphically through textured drawings, collage, castings etc and verbally through definition, metaphor, alliteration and character-ization. They sought relationships of engagement that could be expounded upon at multiple scales and directed toward different programmatic components, sites and materials. Their ability to operate the fly as a *lure* in the cultivation of landschaft was the hermeneutic goal. As the studio progressed, the importance of the lure gave way to each student's internal ideology. The images presented here testify toward ways of repositioning the production of landscape through pointed personal and social logics. This is true not only for the actual landscape but for the rhetorical as well. The role of intention, interpretation, certainty, revelation and representation became the cornerstone agents for our architectural pragmatics. The demonstrated operational strategies championed landscape as a dynamic activity—a verb.

Neal Robinson

End Notes:

[1] Jorgen Dehs, "Sense of Landscape. Reflections on a Concept, a Metaphor, a Model," in Surroundings Surrounded. Essays on Space and Science, Peter Weibel, ed. (Cambridge, Mass.: MIT Press 2001), p 169.

306090 04 03|03

306090, Inc.

pp. 102-109 "Speculate Mediate Activate" ©2003 Elise Shelley et al, Published by 306090, Inc.

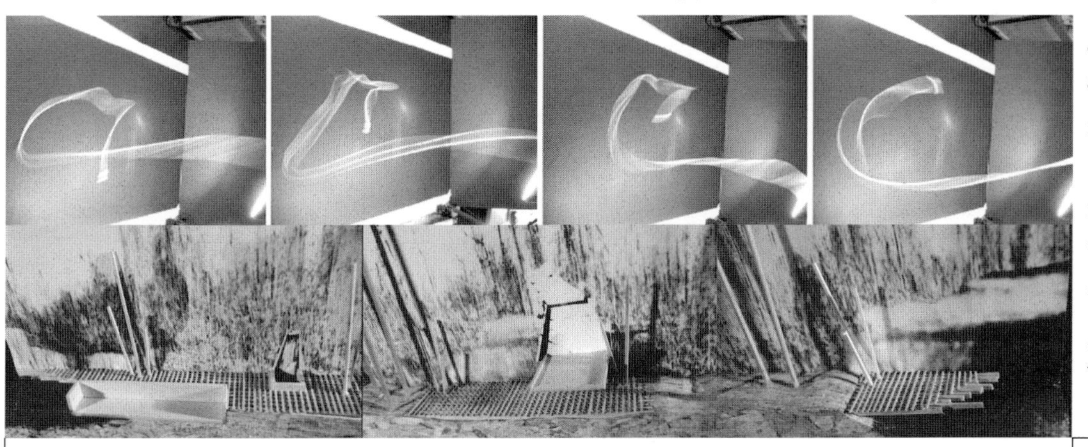

Jeong Han: Casting practice [top]
Amanda Spicuzzi: Plane of production

TOWARDS A NEW

Ellinger/Yehia Design

Structural Roof Geometry

EYe Design explores architecture through a multi-scalar material process

TECHNIQUE

by Jefferson Ellinger and Nona Yehia

Both the practice and the discipline of architecture are in the midst of far-reaching change as they are being reshaped, restructured and rescaled by the rapid impact of new technologies. Although it is impossible to foresee the ultimate consequence of this change; it is possible to identify opportunities for a renegotiation of technology's role in design. This approach necessarily embodies an increasingly global notion of making: one that creates a potential shift in contemporary architectural practice where the development of a productive technique is placed at a greater value than that of image. As the novelty of computer-generated design continues to fade, a critical reevaluation of the role of the computer during the process of design needs to take place. To this end, a "second generation" of digital architects and theorists is emerging: one that places emphasis on the use of technique-driven design by way of utilizing computational and material technologies to challenge and reinvent traditional modes of producing architecture.

Before the Mustache

The fundamental design principles which facilitated the emergence of 'media based' architectural design and digital practices have been all but forgotten. At the heart of these principles is the development of a new logic for the production of form: fundamentally, this could be articulated as

EYe Design, founded in 2000 by Jefferson Ellinger and Nona Yehia, has positioned itself as an innovative design laboratory specializing in design technique manifest through digital processes. They are in the process of writing a book entitled Material Technique that critiques the nature of architectural practice and presents a multidisciplinary alternative driven by new methods of producing and manufacturing.

The firm was recently chosen as a finalist in the MOMA/PS1 Young Architects Competition for 2003. Nona Yehia and Jefferson Ellinger both graduated from Columbia University, NY in 1997 and worked for Reiser+Umemoto, Greg Lynn Form and Eisenman Architects. Jefferson currently is a Clinical Professor of Architecture at Rensellear Polytechnic Institute in Troy, NY.

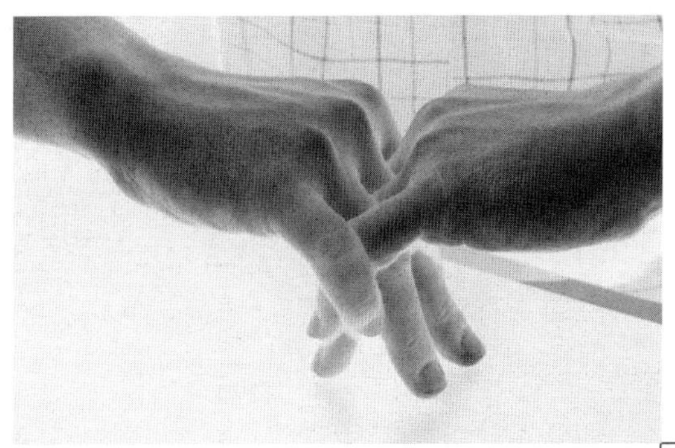

< Weaving Concept

306090 04 03 | 03

Published by 306090, Inc.

pp. 110–115 "Towards a New Technique" ©2003 Jefferson Ellinger + Nona Yehia,

the difference between a line and a spline. Unlike a line, which merely connects two points, a spline or vector based geometry constantly updates its shape based on the influence of three or more loci typically called control vertices. As these control vertices (cv's) change, the geometry of the spline adapts recursively across itself to produce a shape that has this new information embedded within it. Because of the numeric complexity of these spline geometries the computer became the only efficient tool for designing with them. Further, time based operations could influence or mutate the information, and ultimately the geometry, giving the project a temporal or fourth dimensional element of intelligence. Therefore a technique developed to allow for difference to become an active agent in producing informed geometric novelty, ultimately leading to formally complex geometries. [1]

Construction < > Design

However, it became increasingly clear that the materialization of these geometries was compromised for two distinct reasons. First, traditional methods of building and documentation (namely, the linear flow of information from architect to engineer to contractor) did not allow for complex geometric descriptions to be communicated adequately. Second, without constraint, the medium of computer generated design is completely plastic and without material limitation. This fact necessitated re-designing complex forms to adhere to typical construction techniques. So in many cases the work simply was either produced though traditional methods of construction, or remained within the realm of the virtual or became purely ornamental.

While there is no doubt that the latter issues of ornamentation and the realm of the virtual can be considered architectural, it is debatable whether these mediums can be considered Architecture. Rather than engaging that debate here, the crucial issue of how to adapt building techniques to the new design environment should be pursued. Manual De Landa categorizes the act of making or "genesis of form" as emanating from one of two distinct philosophies of design. (The first is "primarily conceptual or cerebral, something to be generated as a pure thought in isolation" that then have materiality applied to them. The second is "represented by a philosophy of design in which materials are not inert receptacles for a cerebral form…, but active participants in the genesis of form.") [2] Implied in this statement is an understanding of intrinsic (real) material properties; the shaping forces of design. This necessitates infusing the real physical properties of a material technique to influence design trajectories; adding the tactile material tolerances absent from the

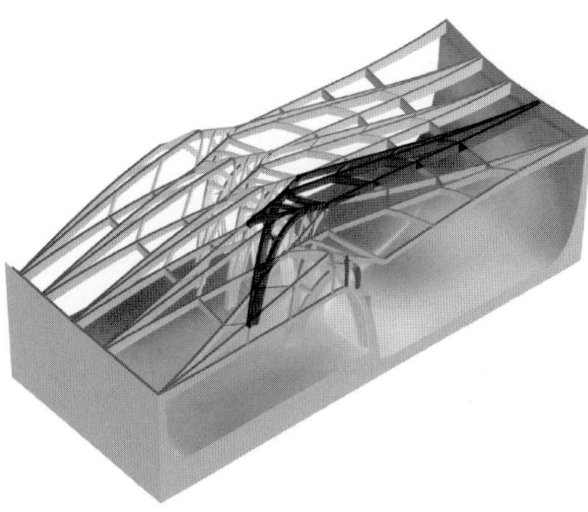

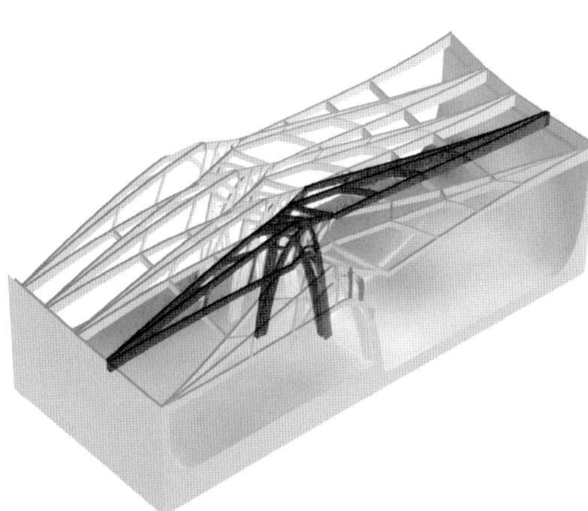

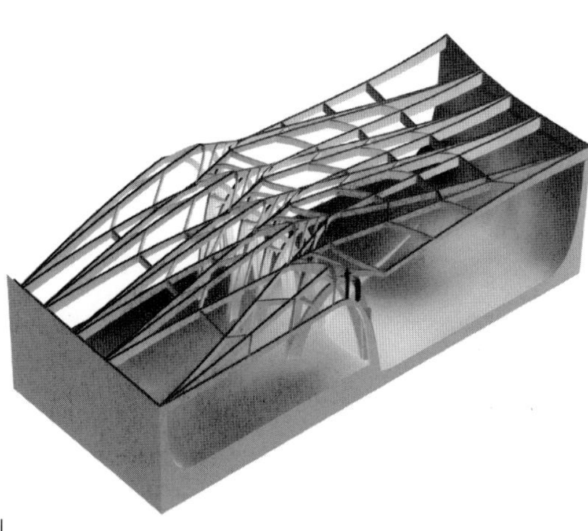

computer. Bastardizing intention for the sake of archaic construction techniques falls short of the designer's potential, and reduces novelty to the realm of the image. This image-making became so completely seductive as an unrealizable project that the fundamental design logics of computational technologies have been lost and for the most part, it is this self referential plastic image of computer generated architecture that has proliferated, rather then the generative technique.

Recursive Processes

Reinvestigating the entire practice of making through a similar digital process would allow for truly novel architecture to emerge. Rather than restricting or limiting operations to geometric (formal) manipulations, the process, or more precisely the technique should be expanded to include material implications. The word 'material' not only refers to the physicality of the architecture, but also to the material implications of the collaborative process that is architecture; designers, engineers, manufacturers, clients, contractors, local building agencies and practices, etc. It is important to no longer fetishize the computer as the design catalyst for form generation, but rather understand it for what it is; another tool in the toolbox. This is not to deny the importance of the computer, but rather to say that, like any tool, it has a specific usefulness as well as specific shortcomings. The computer is a device with virtually no numerical limitation, meaning that an unlimited amount of empirical data can now be analyzed. Using computational devices to develop a design is not an entirely new idea in architecture. It can easily be argued that Antonio Gaudi utilized extremely efficient and complex, although restrictive, computational devices in the design of his work; specifically the catenary models used in designing Sagrada Familia. As has been well documented, using the catenary curve as a design technique was extremely useful because it gave Gaudi the precise shape for structuring this project. However, what is more interesting is the fact that he would alter or manipulate the shape of a curve by adding additional weights to a given curve. In a similar way that a spline reconfigures its geometry based on the numerical weight and location of its' cv's, the literal weights in Gaudi's model would reinform the shape of the string, sending swells of influence through the entire string network, while maintaining a precise structural stability. With this computational system Gaudi could then redistribute weights across the project to achieve desired architectural effects. Inherent within this design technique is the material issue of making to produce a desired effect so that, in the end, the resultant project is part of the evolution of this technique rather than a residual image of a digital process.

306090 04 03 | 03

Published by 306090, Inc.

©2003 Jefferson Ellinger + Nona Yehia

pp. 110-115 "Towards a New Technique"

Given this, the importance then clearly lies in prioritizing the content of the data (what the data is) and the technique used (how the data is manipulated) in that analysis. Within a digital practice, the computer would then become an agent for negotiation during the design of the project, actively allowing multiple influences to fluidly re-inform the design in a technique driven system that can incorporate change productively. Difference is then implemented as a useful and necessary reorganizer of material and form in the medium of duration, producing a truly novel and efficient end product.

This may sound like the classic design process of iteration, but is actually quite different. Rather, it is the way in which a designer can embed a logic into a project so that it is ready and indeed eager for modification. This new project is not dependant on deviation through repetition for change, but instead on accepting new information as opportunistic moments for adaptation and evolution through mutation. This process of "becoming-ever-different"[3] could incorporate methodologies such as the use of computer-aided manufacturing to produce a variable tectonic that would adapt to local programmatic and structural constraints that then, much like in a feedback loop, ripple back through a projects materialization, via intention, to affect a buildings presence.

K House

The process in which the K House was designed can be seen as a model for this new material process. An initial roof surface was developed as a sketch idea with programmatic and spatial effects. Simultaneously, as the project continued to develop, tectonic systems were quickly folded into the design. Primarily because of technological constraints (limiting size of members produced via available CNC machinery), the structure was developed as a performatively hybrid bay system that is at once structurally stable as a spanning and columnar element. To develop this construction logic further, an uniformed structural prototype was developed. The lines of the major structural system weave or knuckle through themselves to produce a laterally stable frame which is then infilled or locally articulated with more formally complex geometric elements, all of which are to be produced using computer aided manufacturing. This produced an unexpected effect that reinforced the surface complexity as the variegated module would become denser in complex areas and loosen in the areas of sweeping surfaces, which was then rearticulated through the *scalloped* geometries of the infill elements. This structural sketch was then broken down into four modules. Size was determined by material costs, structural integrity and joint limitations as constraints that were then

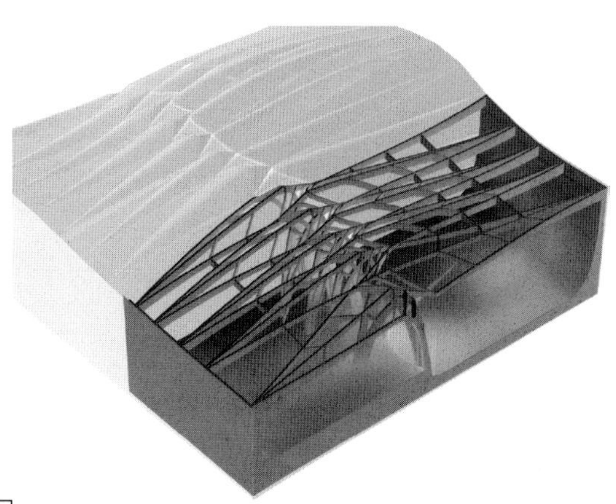

While globalization might be seen as a homogenizing agent, it is registering difference by taking on the intrinsic properties of local components

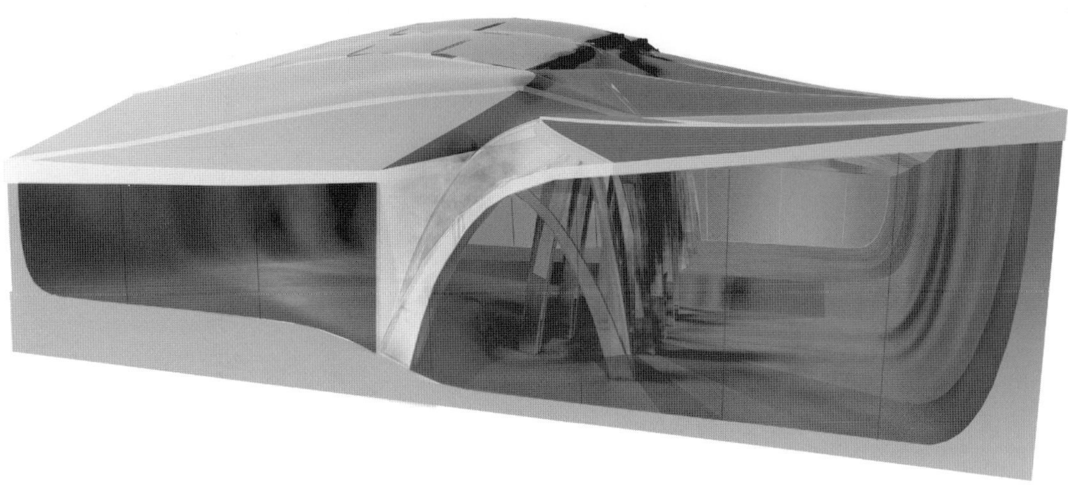

inputted as part of the design criteria. (images: section of weaving structure, two-interwoven bays and components of the bay system). Models were manufactured and tested through material trials; each time reshaping and resizing the elements of the prototype. As this material system was executed in the design of the house, a constraint feed back of information rippled back through the project; recursively altering and reconfiguring the tectonic and spatial effect to produce an architecture that is 'becoming ever different'.

Material Technique

The practice of architecture itself can be seen as a material, where the "emergent whole(s) arises(ing) from the interactions between many components"[4]. Like the Material Scientist, who inherently operates in a multidisciplinary fashion—negotiating with chemists, physicists, and engineers, the architect must do the same. In the same way that as a material undergoes a phase transition under varying conditions results in radically different material properties; an architect must go through similar shifts when the contextual and local elements are altered.

While global interconnectedness has dominated and altered most disciplines through the implementation of new technologies, architecture as a discipline has isolated itself from expansion into the global network by maintaining its autonomous position where design is "a pure thought in isolation"[5]. As the second generation of digital architects is impelled to take on work at a global scale, it is through the material lens that scalar[6] novelty develops. While globalization might seem to be a homogenizing agent, it is registering difference by taking on the intrinsic properties of local components allowing the architect to shift from being solely the author to becoming an active organizer or conductor.

End Notes:

[1] These notions of how a spline geometry can embody information stem from conversations with Greg Lynn, and are reinforced through his work. See Greg Lynn. Folds, Bodies and Blobs, Collected Essays, (Books-By-Architects, 1998)

[2] Manuel Delanda. "Philosophies of Design, The Case of Modeling Software." In Verb, Architecture Boogazine (Aktar 2000). p 132

[3] Sanford Kwinter. Architectures of Time, Toward a Theory of the Event in Modernist Culture. (The MIT Press, 2001) p 4.

[4] Manuel Delanda. "Philosophies of Design, The Case of Modeling Software." In Verb, Architecture Boogazine (Aktar 2000). p 142.

[5] Ibid, p 132.

[6] In this sense scaler novelty refers to teasing specificity out of local conditions (local regulating agencies; local construction practices; social, economic and cultural forces; and local infrastructures) that recursively transmit across regional and global networks.

306090 04 03 | 03 115

pp. 110-115 "Towards a New Technique" ©2003 Jefferson Ellinger + Nona Yehia, Published by 306090, Inc.

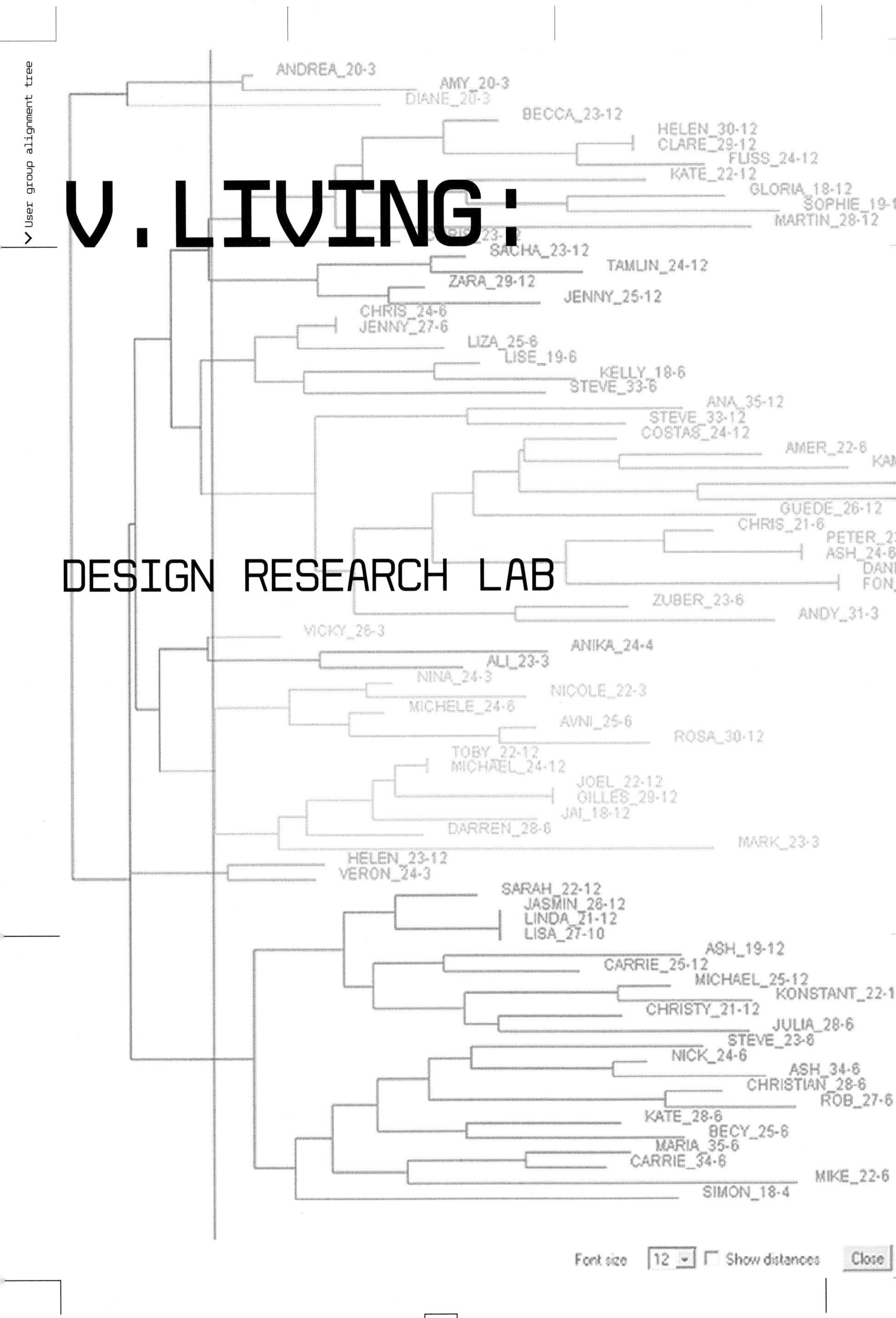
V.LIVING:
DESIGN RESEARCH LAB
User group alignment tree
ANDREA_20-3
AMY_20-3
DIANE_20-3
BECCA_23-12
HELEN_30-12
CLARE_29-12
FLISS_24-12
KATE_22-12
GLORIA_18-12
SOPHIE_19-1
MARTIN_28-12
SACHA_23-12
TAMLIN_24-12
ZARA_29-12
JENNY_25-12
CHRIS_24-6
JENNY_27-6
LIZA_25-6
LISE_19-6
KELLY_18-6
STEVE_33-6
ANA_35-12
STEVE_33-12
COSTAS_24-12
AMER_22-6
KAM
GUEDE_26-12
CHRIS_21-6
PETER_2
ASH_24-6
DANI
FON_
ZUBER_23-6
ANDY_31-3
VICKY_26-3
ANIKA_24-4
ALI_23-3
NINA_24-3
NICOLE_22-3
MICHELE_24-6
AVNI_25-6
ROSA_30-12
TOBY_22-12
MICHAEL_24-12
JOEL_22-12
GILLES_29-12
JAI_18-12
DARREN_28-6
MARK_23-3
HELEN_23-12
VERON_24-3
SARAH_22-12
JASMIN_26-12
LINDA_21-12
LISA_27-10
ASH_19-12
CARRIE_25-12
MICHAEL_25-12
KONSTANT_22-1
CHRISTY_21-12
JULIA_28-6
STEVE_23-6
NICK_24-6
ASH_34-6
CHRISTIAN_28-6
ROB_27-6
KATE_28-6
BECY_25-6
MARIA_35-6
CARRIE_34-6
MIKE_22-6
SIMON_18-4
Font size 12 Show distances Close

Five operations on domestic urbanism uncover the interface of architecture and urbanism

306090 04 03 | 03

pp. 116-125 "V.LIVING" ©2003 Lawrence Sassi et al, Published by 306090, Inc.

by Alan Dempsey, Paul L.Loh, Lawrence Sassi, Lorenzo Viola

Operations in Domestic Urbanism

V. Living is a model of domestic urbanism predicated on the possibility of defining architectural and urban interventions as a condition of interface. Specifically articulated for temporary residents in central London, the model aims to integrate commercial products and services into distributed domestic facilities. Existing definitions of public and private space are reformulated as an active negotiation between the movement of different user groups and the products and services mobilized by their interaction. Through observation and analysis of this movement, V. Living investigates the trajectories of interaction between residents and urban users as conditions of access and change in use over time.

V. Living's preliminary research explored dynamic models of physical and online interface found in central London and experimented with ways in which they can be recorded and simulated. An examination of these processes revealed ways in which the distribution of people, products and services could provide an operative description of contemporary urban dynamics. The Virgin group of companies is a UK based corporation that is already engaged in many of these processes through their various companies including Virgin Atlantic, Virgin Records, Virgin Megastore, Virgin

Project Team:

Alan Dempsey: Dublin Institute of Technology (Dip. Arch.), Trinity College, Dublin (BS in Architecture), Architectural Association (MArch) Educated in Dublin, Ireland, Bogotá, Columbia and London, UK. Alan has been an invited critic at the Architectural Association Intermediate School, the Design Research Lab, Pennsylvania State University exchange program, and the Diploma school at the University of East London. When not in the obsessive grip of data streams and drawings he has worked with Ocean and Farjadi Farjadi Architects. Dempsey is currently a 'tourist' in London.

Paul L. Loh: University of Melbourne (BPD), University of East London (Dip. Arch.), Architectural Association (MArch) Born in Malaysia, educated in Melbourne, Australia and London, UK. Loh has taught at the University of East London as design & technical tutor and as invited guest for the URB forum, Venice (2002). He has worked in Malaysia, and Australia is currently working in London and completing an MA in Architecture History & Theory

*Lawrence Sassi Jr: New Jersey Institute of Technology (BArch), Architectural Association (MArch) Born in the Bronx, New York, educated in New Jersey and London. Sassi has been an invited critic at Barnard College, NJIT and the University of East London and has worked on projects by Stephen Holl Architects and most recently for Acconci Studio in NY.
Contact: lawrencesassi@hotmail.com*

Lorenzo Viola: Istituto Universitario di Architettura Politecnico di Milano (Dip. Arch.), Architectural Association (M.Arch.) Born in Milan, Italy, educated in Milan, Italy and London UK. Viola has worked on projects by Kenzo Tange and Takenaka Europe GMBH, Zaha Hadid Architects and most recently for Nicholas Grimshaw & Partners Limited in London.

Mobile, and Virgin Wines among others. Virgin was taken on as a pseudo client for the project. Acting as a preexisting model of distribution and organization, this provided a direction for initial research. Specifically, some preliminary research topics included the distribution of Virgin commercial outlets and temporary accommodation in central London, public use of the mobile phone, virginwines.com and on-line dating services.

The increasing mobility and migratory nature of urban populations has forced products, services, and facilities to become mobilized, thus transcending existing definitions of use, function and boundary. This leads to the view that contemporary cities are inherently trajectorial. When considering cities as trajectorial fields it becomes impossible to define intense urban environments in terms of fixed, pre-defined territorial space. Existing definitions of public and private space are no longer adequate in describing urban environments. Public spaces are now temporarily actualized for private interactions, as can be seen in phenomena ranging from

incessant public use of cellular phones to the personal appropriation of domestic interiors like that of Starbucks. Conversely, public forums have become an assemblage of networked domestic interactions such as online communities and the retail browsing and transactions that take place on sites such as virginwines.com. This dissolution of previously delineated civic space makes it necessary to rethink the city as an interface with flows of movement that are continuously modulating over time.

V. Living addresses the issue of providing housing in such a context. The design proposal engages with the dynamic processes observed in the city and responds to the contemporary lifestyle patterns that engender those processes.

The evolution of the project established a design and research process that took the form of working through a set of five interdependent operations—distribution, user group, structure, interface, movement—that allowed the project to emerge through their continual interaction.

Operation #1—Distribution

V. Living's site strategies make use of London Underground's Central Line to deploy a distributed network of small-scale interventions. Clusters defined by the user group tree diagram can be distributed throughout the site while maintaining connection through circulation and existing site movement. The specific location of interventions around each tube station exploits the logic of existing services already active on site. V. Living would take over the management of these facilities and install additional services as required to sustain an integrated living environment. During normal business hours the services are staffed and open to both resident and urban populations. During hours when the services are normally closed to the public, they are un-staffed and remain open for use by V. Living residents only—i.e. the restaurant becomes your private dining room. V.Living residents—as temporary dwellers in London—enjoy benefits and facilities similar to what might be available in a major hotel environment. The model also actively engages existing circulation infrastructures around tube stations differentiating and redirecting them across multiple installations. Through this engagement our strategy questions established figure/ground relations in favor of a more permeable ground condition that can negotiate between multiple activities and trajectories of movement.

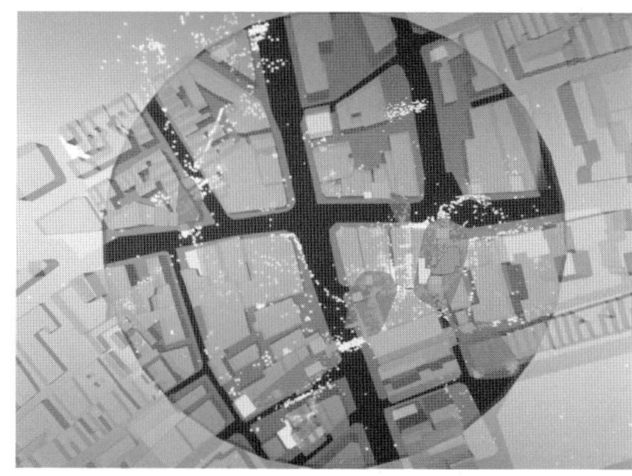

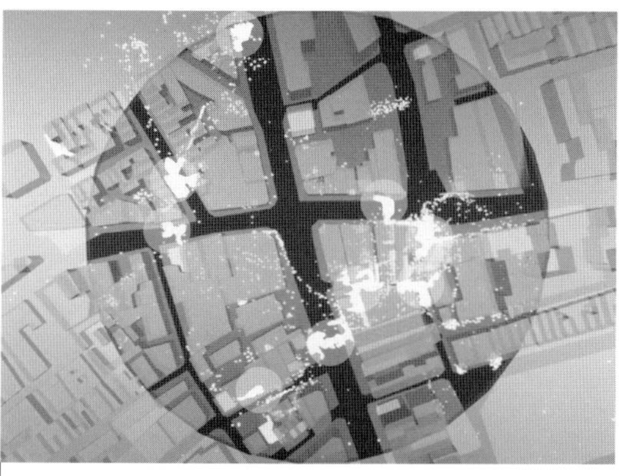

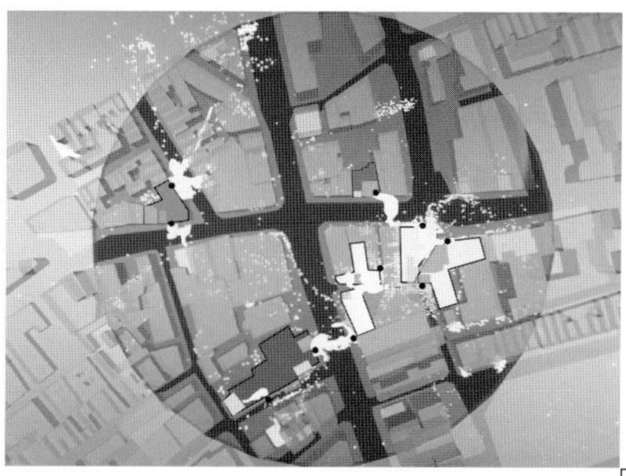

Density radii / defined zones of intervention

Possible permeability /integration of services

306090 04 03 03

pp. 116-125 "V.LIVING" ©2003 Laurence Sassi et al, Published by 306090, Inc.

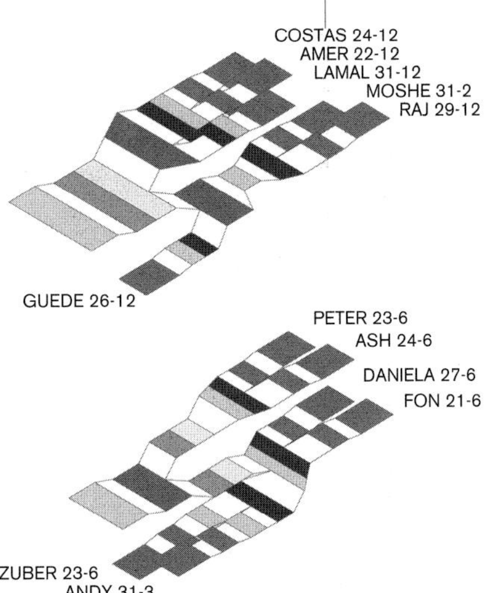

Operation #2—User Group

Speculating from existing models of virtual communities such as on-line dating agencies and flat-share services, V. Living identifies its potential community as single, temporary—0-12 months—urban dwellers. To generate possible living scenarios we identified specific users through advertisements that were placed in print and online offering available, fictitious accommodations. In 14 days we received 333 responses complete with each applicant's personal profile and sharing preferences. Applicants were coded according to the profile and preferences they provided in their responses. Molecular sequence alignment software was then (mis)used to generate groups or clusters based on their similarities. The sequences were aligned by the software and grouped in a nearest neighbor tree. This branching tree structure provides the social organizational model of V. Living and suggests an increasingly differentiated spatial arrangement of the living units from the domestic to the urban. In order to translate the tree diagram it is re-mapped using the possible activities associated with each programmatic spatial sequence to create a diagram of shared, territorial zones of occupation. The user diagrams are finally translated into a distributive surface for each individual apartment, the forms of which are articulated by including information from the distribution and structural operations.

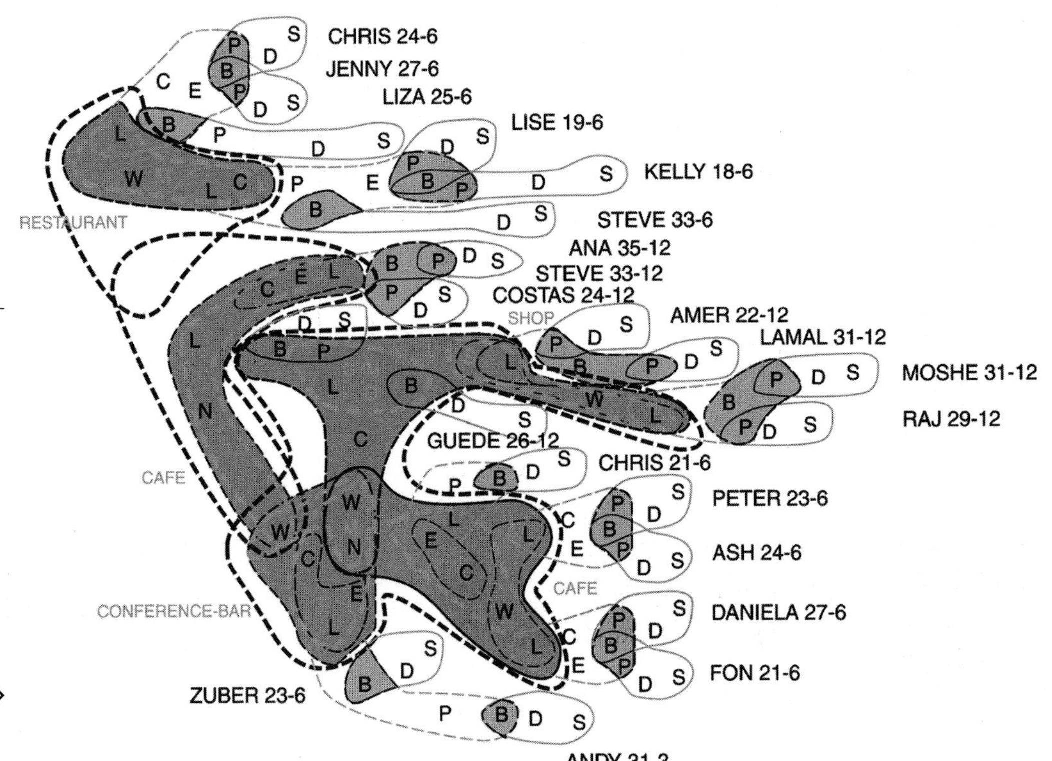

Operation #3—Structure

The structural research investigates flexible material organizations that are capable of integrating with existing urban infrastructures while also being able to accommodate the highly differentiated conditions of new living arrangements. A rule-based proliferation of a single element generates the entire structural system. This proliferation defines architecture and urbanism starting from small scale iterations that ultimately generate surfaces, enclosure systems, and threshold conditions. At its most basic, the proposed system is a highly flexible double weave built up from this single element. Variation in the density of the structure, individual units, and overall configuration respond to site-specific inputs, thresholds configured by the user tree diagrams, diagrams of movement and territorial spaces, and the range and limits of the structural system. As the system of interconnected elements grows it forms a surface that—when differentiated—organizes function and circulation and is instrumental in spatially distributing user movement, services and living units across the site. A single surface has minimal thickness on its own, and so is doubled, offset by 150mm, and then interconnected by the same type of structural element, constructing a structural double skin. This particular configuration allows the system to remain structurally stable while the surface deforms through incremental end rotation of the individual elements.

C

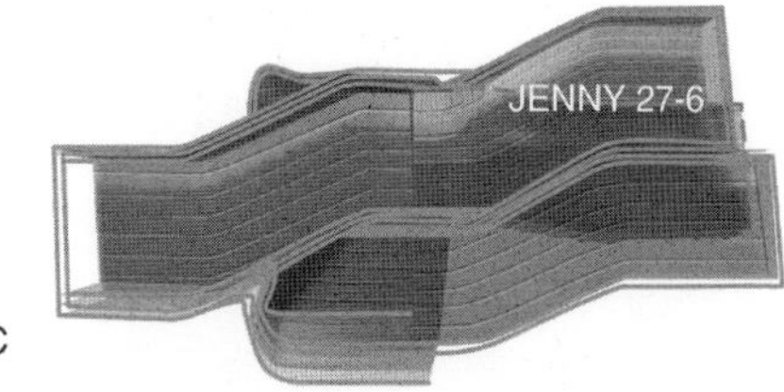

B

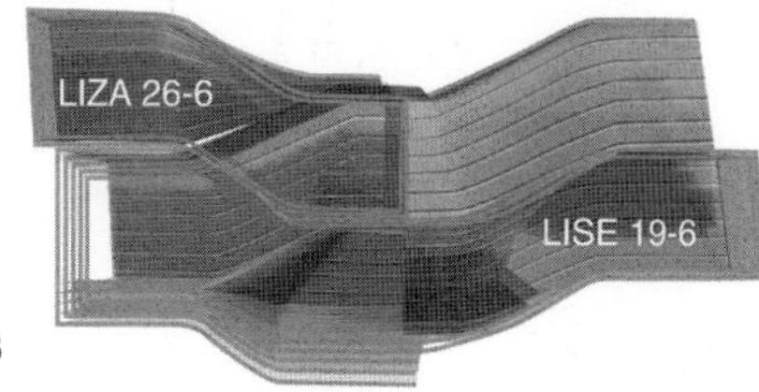

A

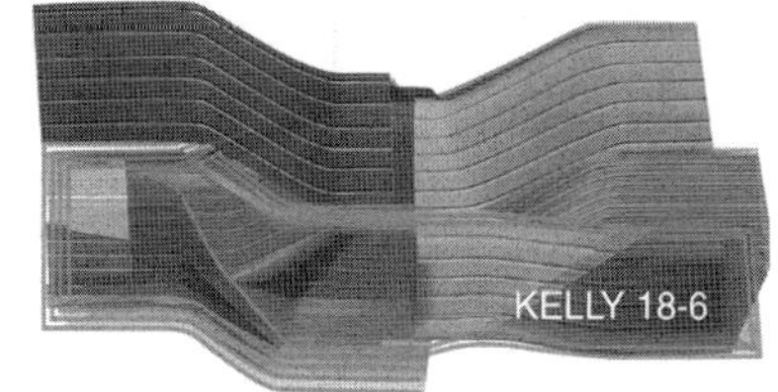

306090 04 03 | 03

pp. 116-125 "V.LIVING" ©2003 Lawrence Sassi et al, Published by 306090, Inc.

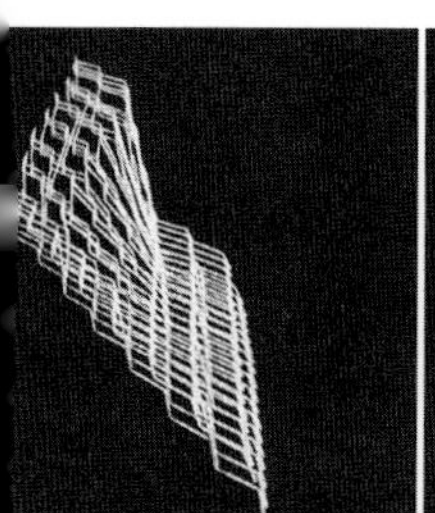
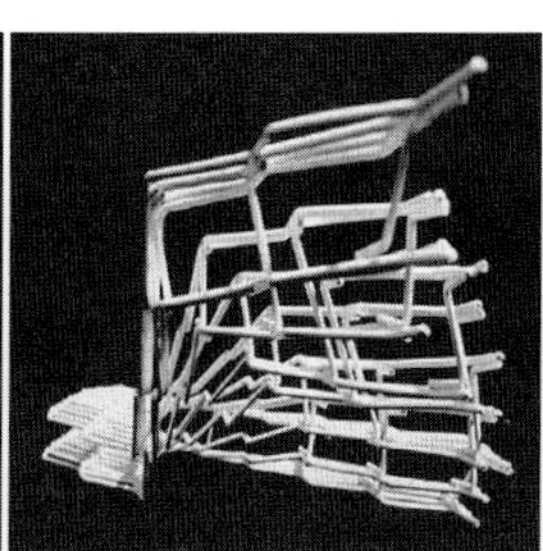
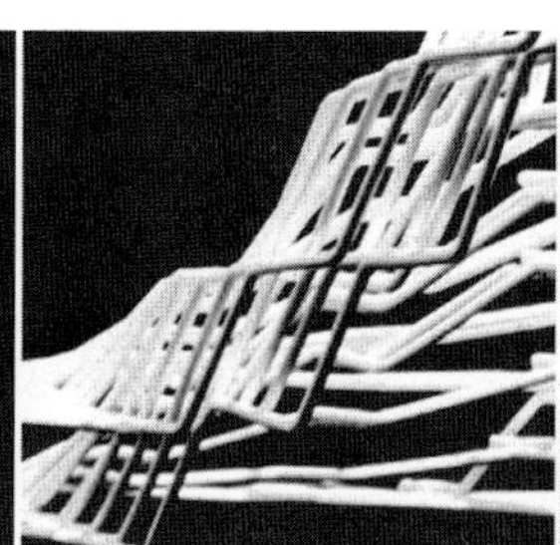
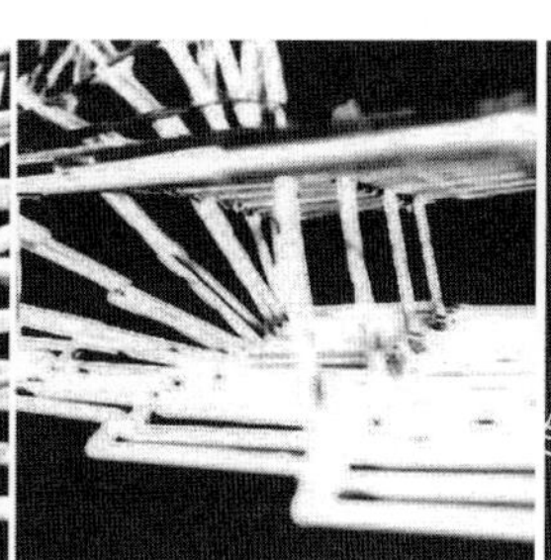
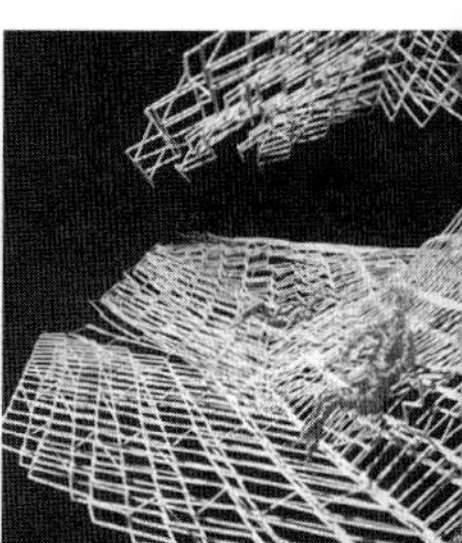

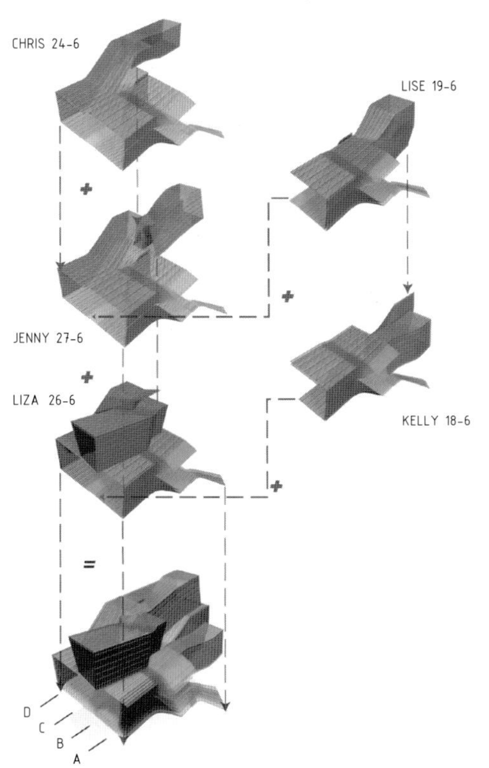

Operation #3 [continued]

A 150mm space between the joined surfaces
of the double skin provides space for plumbing,
mechanical, and electrical systems throughout
the living units. Structural studies present a series
of static actualizations within the rotation of the
elements that deform the surface. Double skin
structural surfaces enclose each of the individual
units at the end of the circulation path on four
sides as floor/wall, and ceiling/wall surfaces. The
overall structural organization of the proposal then
arises from the accumulation of these individual
user surfaces. The 150mm double skins accumulate
as a user moves toward the service areas and
movement trajectories of other residents converge,
increasing the structure's thickness. These multiple
structural skins allow longer spans to accommodate
more people as spaces are shared among residents
and in turn allows each user's territory to be
structurally traced from their respective sleeping
areas to street level.

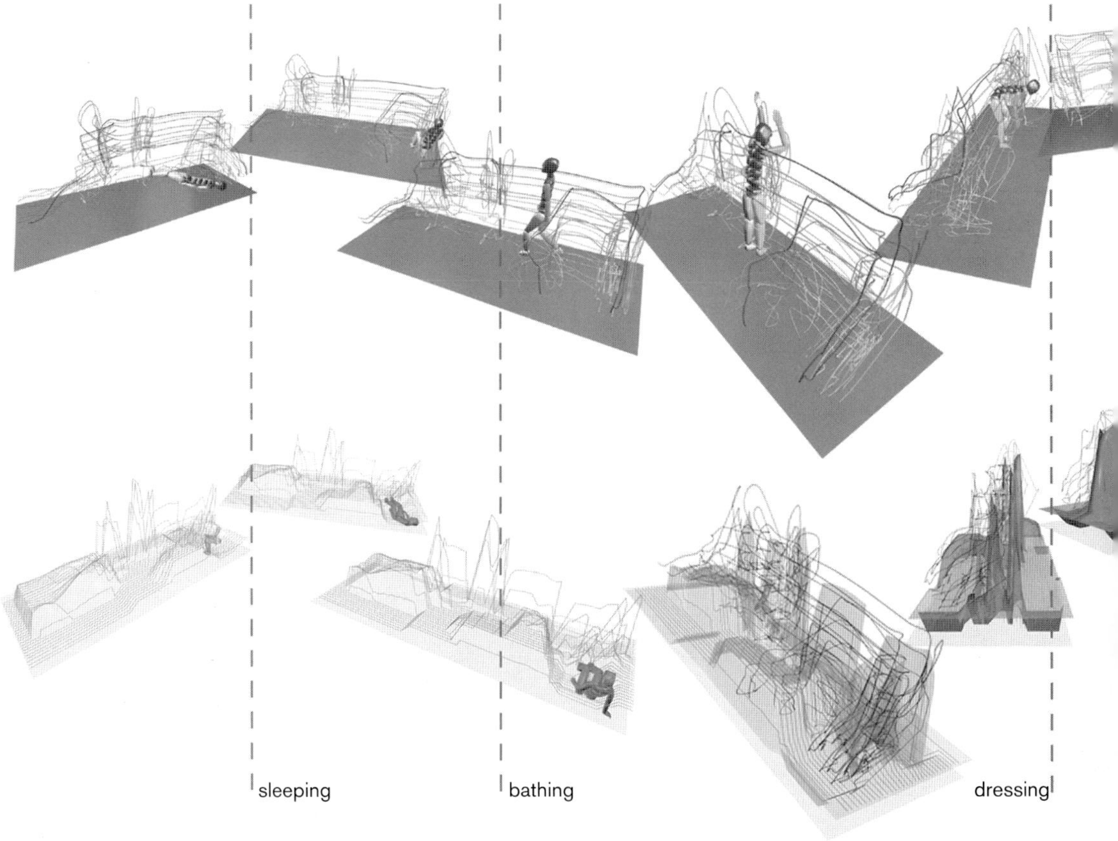

306090 04 03 03

pp. 116-125 "V.LIVING" ©2003 Laurence Sassi et al, Published by 306090, Inc.

Operation #4—Interface

V. Living explores the ergonomic interface of bodies as an interactive and responsive part of the living environment. Our research suggested an ergonomic understanding of a body as being constantly in transition between activities and therefore trajectorial in nature. The research techniques seek to re-define the understanding of the body as a series of interfacing conditions that are distributive, connected fragments. When these conditions are examined in direct relation to the articulation of the structural system it is possible to propose furnishings that engage the complex nature of the performance of the body. Taking an activity sequence from a predefined matrix, we examine the transitional body as it moves from one activity to the next. Pivotal points on the body are recorded as it undergoes a sequence of transformative motions.

The recorded trajectories identify the space-time envelope of the body and indicate a surface of interface around which material could then be configured. The resulting trajectories suggest that the ergonomic transition between activities can function materially as a disruption of a normative field. The surfaces generated map the disruptive spatial moment inherent in the activities sequence. This field produces datum levels that denote points where the body rested when performing a series of possible activities associated with the program space. These disruptions and the datum levels are used to articulate the ergonomic interface of a furnishing typology.

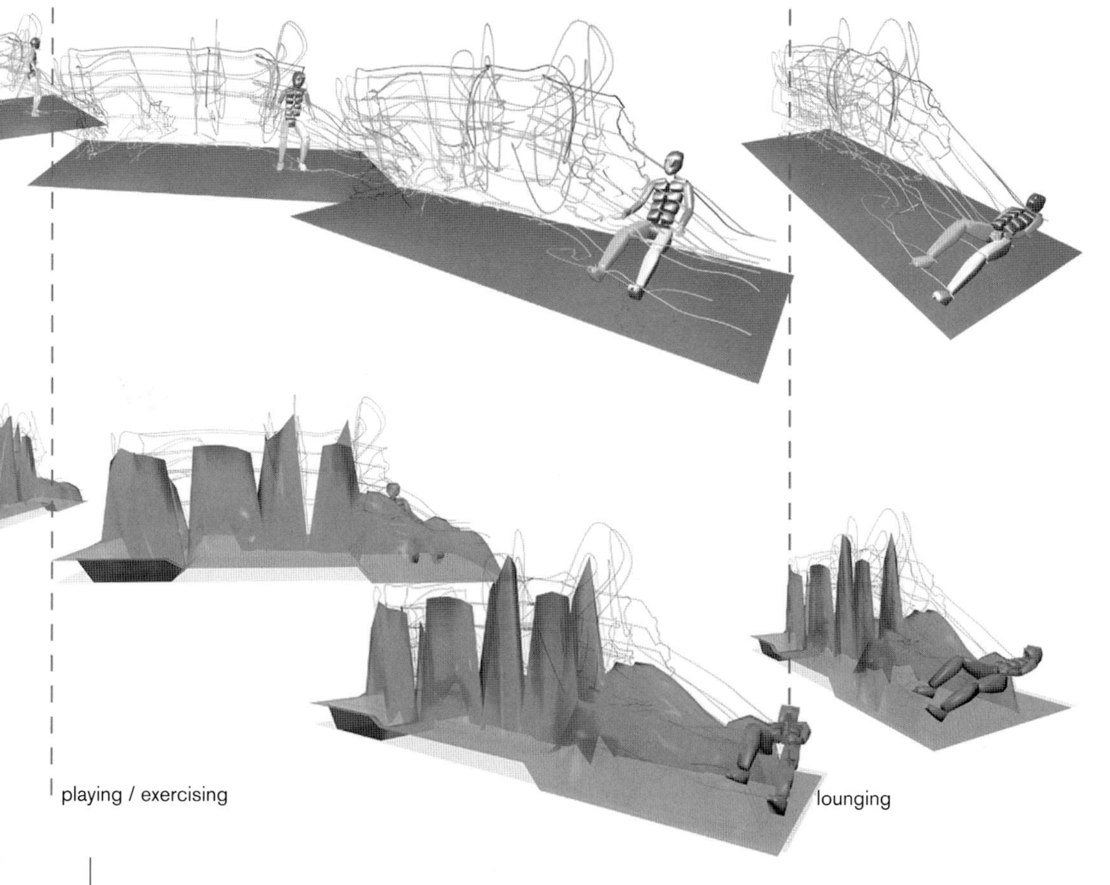

playing / exercising

lounging

Operation #5 - Movement

Through modeling and simulation, this work
develops an understanding of urbanism as an
assemblage of bodies—products, material and
people—as they move through a given environment.
The research concludes that contemporary
urbanism is most accurately described as a series
of interacting trajectories that vary in intensity over
time. Similarly, the project proposes that large-
scale urban interventions can be redefined as an
iterative accumulation of smaller interventions that
have a specified range of variation.The strategy for
intervention must engage with existing trajectories
of localized circulation. V. Living activities can
be installed along these lines of movement,
reconfiguring them as conditions of access to the
proposed intervention.

Afterword

This work documents a Masters Thesis project undertaken at the
Architectural Association Design Research Lab in London. It was
produced during a sixteen-month period and completed in January
2002. What began as a collaborative effort between four people,
shortly developed into a large network of diverse specialists
whose support and consultation were a vital part of the project.
Consultants were integrated into the thesis by providing advice at
periodic meetings, providing material samples, and assisting with
technical advice. Their input was not however limited to their areas
of expertise as they continually engaged all aspects of the proposal
on conceptual, social, and practical levels. With no predetermined
hierarchy or organization, the group had to develop and continually
test strategies that would facilitate a consistent workflow, while
remaining indeterminate enough to encourage ideas to take new
directions.

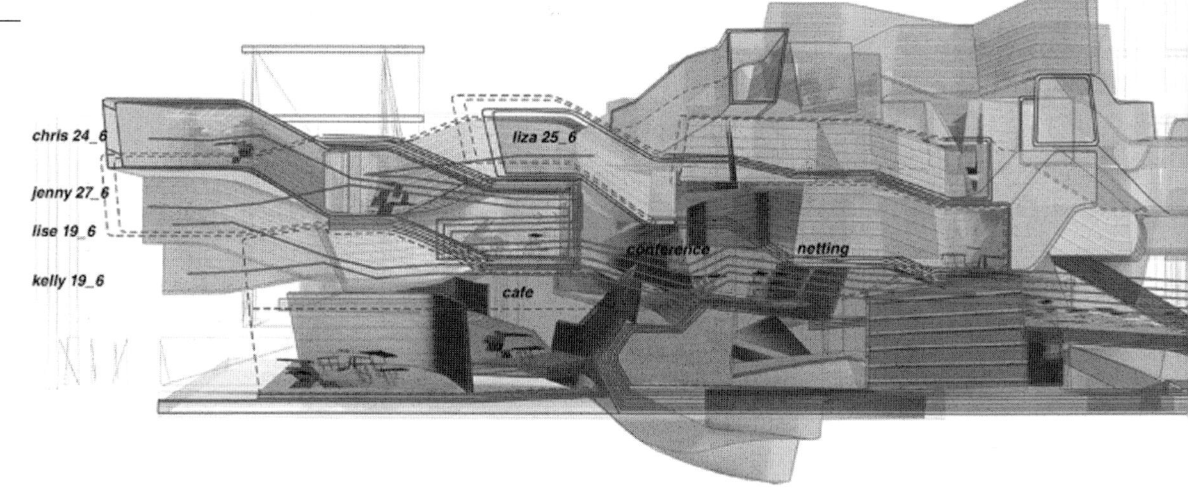

Building section trajectories >

V. Living exploited the research process to address fundamental
questions about architectural practice today, both in the way
architects interact with outside consultants and, more critically,
with one another. Embedded within the working methodology is
a commitment to the investigation of the relationship between
new digital technologies, the design process and contemporary
architectural practice. As it is still in its emergent stages, the
development of digital practices in architecture has few defined
conventions on which to rely. As such the research proceeds
experimentally, with continual testing of digital potentials against
models of physical artifact and material operation. Through
the continual organization and reorganization of material and
information, V. Living sought to examine and expand existing
architectural debate.

By selective appropriation of specific phenomena in seemingly
disparate fields, the project explores new directions and raises
questions about their implications for contemporary architecture.
The following document this process and once again reshuffles a
body of research material to draw out the issues the group believe
to be critical to contemporary architectural discourse.

Program Direction:
Architectural Association Design Research Lab
Directors:
Patrik Schumacher and Brett Steele
with instructors Andrew Benjamin and Chris Hight
Course Master and Advisor:
Tom Verebes

Consultants:
Marcellus Letang: AA Workshop
(cnc modeling coordination and production)
Hanif Kara: Adams Kara Taylor Engineers
(final structural development)
Tom Barker: b consultants (engineers)
(technical assistance with composite skin materials)
David Lewis: Ove Arup and Partners (London)
(development of initial structural concept)
Dr. Heike Laman: Wolfson Institute of Biomedical Research
(molecular sequence alignment assistance)
Dr. Giovanna Lalli: ICRF
(molecular sequence alignment assistance)

Assistants:
Allesandra Sironi, Cedric Libert, Mirco Becket,
Naina Gupta, Simon Kim

306090 04 03 | 03

pp. 116-125 "V.LIVING" ©2003 Laurence Sassi et al, Published by 306090, Inc.

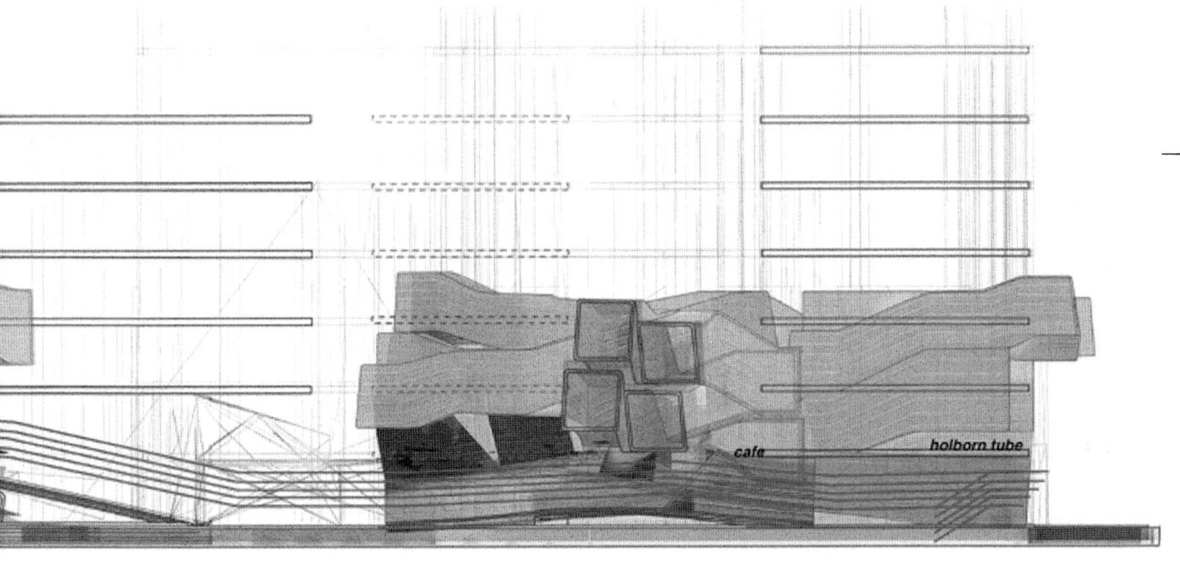

For their generous contributions, 306090 wishes to thank:

The Graham Foundation for Advanced Studies in the Fine Arts
The Richard H. Driehaus Foundation

as well as

Robin Dripps & Lucia Phinney

Princeton University, School of Architecture

University of Virginia, School of Architecture

Renselear Polytechnic Institute

The Hillier Group

The Michael Sorkin Studio

and

M. Christine Boyer

Beatriz Colomina

Claire Flom

Leslie and Peter Flom

Wendy and Jason Flom

David L. Hays

Allen R. Kramer

Margot Krasojevic

Anne R. Kreeger

Nancy Laing

Kevin Lippert

Sadashiv Mallya

Tom & Laura Sandberg

Richard Solomon

306090 04 03 | 03

Jason K. Johnson
Jason received an MArch from Princeton University and a BS from the University of Virginia. He is currently an assistant professor at the University of Virginia and cofounder of future-cities-lab, an interdisciplinary collaborative.
Contact: jasonjohnson@virginia.edu

Nataly Gattegno
Nataly received an MArch from Princeton University and an MA from Cambridge University, UK. She is currently an assistant professor at the University of Virginia and cofounder of future-cities-lab, an interdisciplinary collaborative.
Contact: gattegno@virginia.edu

Alexander F. Briseno
Alex received a MArch and a BS in Architecture from the University of Michigan and has also attended SCI-Arc. He is a designer in New York.
Contact: editors@306090.org

Jonathan D. Solomon
Jonathan Solomon received a BA in Urban Studies from Columbia University and an MArch from Princeton University. He has worked for Michael Sorkin Studio in New York.
Contact: editors@306090.org

Emily A. Abruzzo
Emily received a BA from Columbia University and an MArch from Princeton University. She has worked for SHoP Architects in New York.

Melissa Gronlund
Melissa studied comparative literature at Princeton University and is now an editorial assistant at *ARTnews* in New York.